Sandra Melgar & Other Female Serial Killers

Jessi Dillard

Published by Trellis Publishing, 2021.

SANDRA MELGAR & OTHER FEMALE SERIAL KILLERS

First edition. July 2, 2021.

ISBN: 979-8224324903

Written by Jessi Dillard.

SANDRA MELGAR & OTHER FEMALE SERIAL KILLERS

1

JESSI DILLARD

Two days before Christmas, in 2012, Sandra – or Sandy – Melgar was found tied up inside of a closet in her home in a nice neighbourhood of Houston. A chair was forced against the doorknob, keeping her trapped in the confined space. Her husband Jaime – Jim – Melgar had been stuffed into a different closet – but unlike Sandy, Jim had been killed, first.

A medical examiner's report concluded that Jim had died of blunt force trauma, and multiple stab wounds that had been inflicted with a kitchen knife. The community was horrified, and their horror only grew when police announced that they'd identified the person responsible for the attack on the Melgar family – Sandy Melgar, herself.

Sandy was convicted of killing her 52 year old husband of 32 years, and accused of then staging the entire crime scene to convince police it was a home invasion. But ever since Sandy was locked up in a Texas state prison, her family and her supporters have been fighting to prove that she was wrongfully convicted – the real murderer, the person truly to blame for the brutal slaying of Jim Melgar, is still roaming the streets.

"I know that she did not do this," said Sandy and Jim's daughter, Elizabeth – or Lizz – Melgar Rose, in an interview with 20/20 in November of 2018. "I'm going to fight until we can prove that."

Born in Guatemala, Jim Melgar immigrated with his family to the United States when he was only three years old. They settled in Houston – the same city where a girl named Sandy McCulloch lived. Jim and Sandy attended high school together, and eventually started dating.

According to friends and family, Sandy had initially declined Jim's advances – only relenting when he invited her to come ice skating with him and a group of friends. But when she showed up, it was just Jim and his best friend at the rink, and his friend took off shortly after.

But Jim's sense of humor, intelligence, and thoughtfulness won Sandy over, and two became inseparable in short time. They married when they were only 20 years old, too eager to spend another minute without being man and wife.

Jim pursued a career as an IT specialist, while Sandy studied nursing. They had one daughter, Lizz, and discovered a passion for faith – together, the family joined Jehovah's Witnesses, a Christian denomination that enforces a strict adherence to a specific set of behavioural guidelines.

"We were a very close-knit family," recalled Lizz.

But things weren't perfect. Sandy struggled with a number of health conditions, including lupus, hypothyroidism, and epilepsy. She also underwent hip replacement surgeries.

"She had epilepsy [that began] before I was born, and the lupus didn't come until I was about three," Lizz said. "I remember that because she had to seek treatment for about six weeks. She had gone paralyzed on one side of her body. She was in a wheelchair. She was having a really hard time."

According to family friend Stephanie Davies, Sandy's deteriorating health meant that more and more, Jim was assuming the role of her caretaker.

"Jim was very involved with all aspects – researching her condition, trying to find any kind of possible treatments, cures, whatever he could do," she said. "There were times that she didn't feel safe driving. She was afraid that her seizures might come on ... so she depended on him for a lot of day-to-day activities."

It was the couple's wedding anniversary on December 22, 2012, and they were looking forward to celebrating. Sandy had told her daughter that she and Jim had made plans to have dinner at their favorite Mexican restaurant.

"They stopped by a local CVS just to grab some drink mixers on their way back home," Lizz said, adding Sandy told her that once the couple had gotten home and prepared some cocktails, they headed up to the jacuzzi in their bathroom, where they spent the next few hours.

According to Sandy, their discussions that evening had mostly centered around the time they'd spent together, and their plans for the future. Their intention was to sell the house and use the money to spend the next few years traveling around the world – visiting destinations like Ireland, the Grand Canyon, and somewhere far enough north that they could see the Northern Lights.

Jim was just five months away from retirement, ending his career as a computer programmer with the Houston Independent School District. They'd finally be able to experience everything the world had to offer – and then, Sandy said, they'd discussed purchasing a beach house to settle down in once they'd gotten sick of being on the move.

The family's four dogs had been in the backyard, Lizz said, but according to Sandy, they'd started barking at something after the couple had been in the jacuzzi for about two hours. Sandy told Lizz that Jim had gone downstairs to investigate, and she stayed up in the tub, soaking and finishing her drink.

"I think he took a few minutes, so she decided to get out of the jacuzzi," Lizz relayed. According to what her mother told her, Sandy then went into the closet, sat down on a chair, and began applying lotion to her skin.

The family had planned an anniversary celebration with their entire family for the following day, on December 23. At around 4:30 p.m., Jim's brother, Herman Melgar, showed up with his own family to attend the get-together.

When Herman knocked on the door, there was no answer – no activity of any kind coming from inside the house. But then he noticed one of the garage doors had been left open, so he let himself inside through the access in the garage, looping around to the front door to unlock it for the rest of his family.

They walked through the house, calling for Sandy and Jim, but still got no response.

"I was telling my dad … I remember clearly telling him, 'This doesn't feel right,'" remembers Herman's daughter, Marissa Campos.

It was then that Herman heard something that he thought sounded like a voice. Listening carefully, he figured out that the sound was Sandy Melgar, calling for help from somewhere inside the home. He followed the cries into the master bedroom, where he saw a chair blocking the door from the bathroom to the walk-in closet. Quickly, he pulled the chair out of the way and opened the closet door to find Sandy lying on the floor, her arms and legs tied tightly.

She'd woken up that way, she said – 15 hours after she remembered going into the closet to moisturize her skin. Her muscles ached, her hands and feet were bound, and she'd soiled herself at some point during the night. She had no idea where Jim was.

Herman attempted to pull the ties off her limbs, but couldn't get them loose on his own. Sandy told him to get a pair of scissors to cut them open. With Sandy free, the family began searching for Jim – and it didn't take long to find him.

About 30 feet away from the closet where Herman had found Sandy, Jim Melgar was stuffed in the closet in the master bedroom – daed. He was nude, looked like he'd been beaten, and had been stabbed multiple times. A telephone cord tied his legs together, and a length of rope had also been tied in a loose knot around his chest.

Authorities determined that Jim Melgar's body had sustained more than 50 wounds and injuries, including stabs, cuts, and blunt-force traumas.

"He's got a lot of defensive wounds on both hands, which means he was trying to either disarm the attacker or block the assault," said Celestina Rossi, a prosecution expert witness in the field of blood pattern and crime reconstruction.

According to Rossi, it looked like Jim and his killer had been engaged in hand to hand combat within the closet of the master bedroom, which had eventually resulted in Jim's death right in the room.

"Aside from the 31 cuts and stabs, Jim was badly beaten in the face and head, causing serious damage to his skull, brain, and facial bones," she added.

Jim's wounds were all defensive, according to a medical examiner – the stabbings were concentrated on his chest and hands, with none on his back, indicating he'd attempted to fight off his assailant instead of trying to run away.

As for Sandy, police photographed bruising along her arms, including a particularly intense bruise located on her left bicep. They also documented a small scratch on the thumb of her left hand. However, officers found no blood on any part of Sandy's body.

It appeared that the attack was caused by a home invasion gone wrong. Drawers had been yanked open and torn apart, jewelry boxes had been overturned, and the contents of a wallet and a purse had been spilled out on the bed. In the jacuzzi tub, located right by the master bathroom where Sandy Melgar had been discovered, were a white shirt and a kitchen knife – submerged under the remaining water.

Strangely, though, the locked safe in the bedroom closet where Jim had been killed didn't appear to have been touched. And, even more strangely, authorities also found a loaded gun hidden in the same closet.

As Sandy was the only surviving witness of the incident, police depended on her account of the night's events to determine what had happened to Jim. But it seemed Sandy had a difficult time trying to put together a timeline of the couple's evening.

Her story was relatively similar to the one she'd given her daughter during her interview with police. According to Sandy, she and Jim had celebrated their anniversary with dinner at the Mexican restaurant, and had stopped at CVS on the way home. She claimed she'd noticed a "mysterious car" trailing them from the CVS parking lot, but said that at some point, the vehicle had turned in a different direction.

When they got home, Sandy told detectives, she and her husband had undressed and gotten into the jacuzzi. Then, she said, the dogs started barking the backyard – at around midnight, she believed. Jim had gotten out of the tub to see what had caused the commotion.

"He was just taking a while, so I got out and was going to get dressed, or change in my closet," she said during the interview. "I went in there and I started to change and that's all I remember until I woke up."

At no point did Sandy remember seeing or hearing her husband being attacked by an intruder, she said. It was possible, she told police, that she may have either blacked out after being struck and hitting her head, or she'd suffered an epileptic seizure.

"I couldn't move because I had had a seizure, and so I usually can't move anyway," she'd explained. "I hurt all over and my head hurts."

She also said grand mal seizures leave her feeling very disoriented. Often, she said, she will forget going into it, and when she comes out, she frequently has trouble remembering where she is or what she was doing. In the weeks before the attack, she added, she'd experienced auras, which she said is a symptom that typically warns her of an impending seizure.

But detectives found it hard to believe that anyone could have been completely unaware of their spouse being murdered in the adjacent room. Immediately, according to Sandy's family, she went from being a wife, to a widow, to a suspected murderer in the slaying of her own husband.

"We're gonna find out everything about you," threatened Sheriff Sgt. James Dousay during an interrogation of Sandy Melgar while investigators combed her house. "We're gonna find out everything about your husband. We're gonna talk to everybody in your neighbourhood. We're gonna talk to everybody that you're related to. We're gonna learn everything."

"That'll help you to look somewhere else, too," Sandy replied. "Because it wasn't me."

When Sheriff Sgt. Shawn Carrizal pressed Sandy about the couple's plans for their future, she broke down – leaning forward in her chair, pressing her face into her hands, and sobbing openly. Then, Carrizal started asking her if it was possible that she'd killed her husband.

According to Herman Melgar's daughter, Marissa, detectives had started suspecting her aunt the very night the body was found. However, she said the family finds it hard to believe that after more than 30 years of being happily married, Sandy would suddenly snap and stab her husband dozens of times.

"This idea that something must have happened, and then she went crazy and subjected him to over 50 blunt-force and sharp-force injuries is just... impossible," said Sandy's defense attorney Mac Secrest.

Still, the thought that her mother had murdered her father did cross Lizz's mind.

"I tried to look at the evidence. ... I tried to be unbiased about it, which is difficult because these are my parents," Lizz admitted. "In the end, I still want justice for my dad. I want to know who did this, and it was not my mother."

Despite the interest from police, Sandy Melgar wasn't initially arrested for her husband's murder. For the next year and a half, she tried to move on from the incident and build a life without Jim. Until the summer of 2014, when Lizz said she found out that there was a warrant out for her mother's arrest – Sandy had been indicted in the murder of Jim Melgar.

"We called the lawyer and we had her turn herself in," Lizz said.

Three years later, the case was finally brought to a trial. Prosecutor Colleen Barnett presented the jury with what she claimed was Sandy's motive – she wanted a divorce, Barnett said, but was worried that her fellow Jehovah's Witnesses would shun her, since the religion doesn't allow for divorce.

In a 2018 interview with KHOU News, Barnett admitted she knew the case would be a tough one to argue – the evidence linking Sandy to the crime was entirely circumstantial, and there was no clear motive or confession. However, she believed she was up to the task.

"It was a challenging case, but one I believed in," she said.

Sandy's attorneys, however, put forward a completely different image of the couple – one of happily married parents who were celebrating more than three decades together.

According to the prosecution, Sandy had persuaded Jim to let her tie his legs with the telephone cord, likely in some kind of sexual act. Then, Barnett told the jury, she'd surprised him by pulling out the large kitchen knife and using it to stab him to death.

But the crime scene looked like a home invasion, Barnett said, so Sandy must have taken the time to prepare the room for the authorities that would eventually respond. It was clearly staged, she argued, showing the jury images of drawers that had been "neatly arranged" and not dumped at random, as a real robber would have done. There was also no sign of forced entry, Barnett said.

She also claimed nothing had been taken from the home, but Sandy's defense team argued the opposite, telling the jury several items of value had been removed during the ransacking.

But how had Sandy Melgar wound up stuffed in a closet, with her hands tied behind her back? The jury was presented with a recording officers had made, demonstrating how Sandy could have carefully slid the chair into place through the use of a pillow sham or a small rug, tucking it under the door knob and leaving her locked inside the closet. Barnett, for her part, showed to the jury the steps Sandy might have taken to tie her own hands behind her back, once she'd gotten the chair in place.

Sandy's medical records indicated that she hadn't reported a single seizure to her physician in the years leading up to her husband's death –

in fact, Barnett told the jury, it wasn't until after Jim had been murdered that Sandy began remembering any seizures she'd had that year.

The defense, however, presented the jury with a question that had remained unanswered: what had happened to Jim Melgar's blood? With the series of blunt-force and stab wounds he had sustained, he would have lost a considerable amount of blood – but according to Sandy's defense attorney's, not a single drop of Jim Melgar's blood was found on Sandy's hands. There was also no evidence to indicate that anyone had cleaned up any blood spilled inside of the home. And not only were Sandy's hands clean, they were free of any minor injuries that might have resulted from a struggle with her husband – she didn't even have a chipped or broken nail.

Investigators also discovered DNA on various surfaces within the house – including handles on the dresser drawers, closet doors, and bathroom door – that belonged to a male and female, but didn't match any member of the Melgar family. According to the defense, that DNA was left behind by the unknown assailants that had attacked the couple.

Secrest also told the jury about issues with one of the case's lead investigators, who was later fired from his position after it was discovered that he'd backdated a search warrant for a different murder investigation.

Over the course of two days, the jury spent approximately eight hours deliberating over the case.

"We all talked about how this case... was the last thing you thought about when you went to bed at night, and the first thing you thought about when you woke up in the morning," said Tom Bush, the jury foreman for the trial. "That's the gravity that we weighed this case with."

Initially, according to Bush, the jury was evenly divided. However, by the second day, it had landed on a unanimous verdict: Sandy Melgar was guilty in the murder of her husband, Jim Melgar.

"You know, I felt like ... everything just got really quiet," Lizz recalled. "The room was just kind of spinning. Yeah, I still feel sick to my stomach when I think about it or hear other people talk about it."

Marissa also had a difficult time accepting the jury's verdict, and tried to silently communicate that before leaving the courtroom.

"I remember clearly just looking at the jurors, just staring at them, every single one of them, because I wanted to remember their faces and I wanted them to look at us and see ... the pain that they were causing," she said.

Sandy was sentenced to 27 years behind bars in a Texas state prison, but is appealing the conviction. One month after the jury had rendered its verdict, Secrest filed a motion requesting a new trial, claiming Sandy's conviction had been the result of an "inept investigation" done by detectives who were "clearly theory driven," with "insufficient" evidence to justify the jury's verdict.

"The prosecution's case was based on conjecture and hypotheses, which were not rooted in evidence," he said. "Sandy didn't kill Jaime."

The motion was denied, but the defense intends to continue with the appeals process and prove Sandy's innocence. However, according to Sandra Guerra Thompson, the director of the Criminal Justice Institute at the University of Harvard Law Center, appeals courts traditionally side with the jury – the odds of Sandy Melgar winning her appeal are somewhere between one and two percent.

Thompson, who researches cases of wrongful conviction, said successfully proving a wrongful conviction usually requires that the case attracts outside interest. Which is exactly what the family has been doing. They reached out to Bob Ruff – a former fire chief who now hosts a podcast, "Truth and Justice," which investigates criminal cases.

"You're innocent until proven guilty. I saw that the prosecution's case didn't have any meat to it. There were no bones behind why they convicted her," said Ruff about the Melgar case. "Can I see a scenario where this happened? Can I make this make sense? That Sandra Melgar killed her husband. In this case, I couldn't see it, so we jumped in."

According to Ruff, potential assailants had an opportunity to enter the house without forcing their way in while Jim was out checking on the dogs. Sandy had also stated she wasn't sure if the back door had even been locked that day – it was possible the attackers were already inside the home when the couple returned from their dinner.

"The offenders could have entered through the door, causing the dogs to bark," Ruff posited on his podcast. "Jim emerged from the master suite to check on the dogs. Jim locks the door behind him, and turns around [to see the offenders] confronting him with some kind of weapon."

Lizz said she is pleased to have the support of Ruff and his podcast listeners as the family seeks to have Sandy released from prison, and believes the real perpetrator – the person who actually killed her father – is still walking free.

While Barnett stated she is skeptical of the methods Ruff uses to pursue his investigation, she admitted there is still some question as to Sandy Melgar's guilt.

"I think that people who aren't in law enforcement and haven't seen the evidence ... have a question about it because she walked around with a cane. She's a petite woman. They were married for 32 years. I understand the questions that they have," she said. "It's unusual, for sure, that we have a suspect that's like Sandra. ... But that doesn't determine whether somebody commits a crime or not."

The case has also attracted the attention of another high-profile investigator – attorney Kathleen Zellner, who served as the defense lawyer for Steven Avery during the second series of the popular Netflix documentary Making a Murderer.

"This is huge for us. I'm very excited and very hopeful this is going to lead to an overturned conviction," Lizz told KHOU News following the announcement in December 2018. "I just hope that we can get some justice and start moving forward with life the best we can, and we finally get to grieve my dad like we should have been able to from the beginning."

Zellner immediately announced her intention to retest DNA evidence, as well as additional evidence which she claimed had never been originally examined. The Harris County District Attorney's Office told KHOU it would "cooperate with Kathleen Zellner, as we would with any defense lawyer representing a client."

For Sandy, who spent the first months of her confinement living a very structured life in a six by ten foot prison cell in the William P. Hobby Unit, coming to terms with the death of her spouse has been made incredibly difficult by the fact that she has been blamed for it.

"Sometimes, I think I'm going to go home. I still think, 'I want to tell him this,' and I forget he's gone," she admitted in an 2018 interview with KHOU News. "I don't feel like he's really gone; I just feel like he's temporarily gone or just on a trip out of town. I try not to think of..." She paused, briefly lost in thought. "I know I will see him again."

Her family and friends have remained staunchly on Sandy's side throughout the ordeal, and have even coordinated weekly visits to ensure not a weekend goes by where Sandy doesn't spend her two hours of visitation with some of her loved ones.

In 2018, Sandy submitted a request to be relocated to a medical unit, where she can receive better treatment for her epilepsy and lupus, which was approved. Lizz said it's clear that the experience has taken a toll on her mother.

"I've never seen my mom so broken and devastated, and she never recovered after that. She's never going to be the same person," Lizz said. "She will always have this hole in her life. I just can't put into words how this has affected her, because it's been such a tremendous loss."

KRISTEN GILBERT

LYNN DILMAN

In the early 1990s, former Veterans Affairs (VA) nurse Kristen Gilbert was found guilty of murdering four of her patients – and convicted of attempting to murder two more. Gilbert is suspected to be responsible for the deaths of dozens more veterans who were under her care during her career as a nurse.

"Gilbert is a calculating predator," read an article in the October 8, 2000 edition of the Boston Globe, "nothing less than a serial murderer in a white lab coat who attacked her victims in at the Department of Veterans Affairs Medical Centre here with needles of poison. She struck, [prosecutors] say, as sick veterans lay in high-tech beds provided by their grateful government."

"Twisted, but not stupid."

Born to parents Richard and Claudia Strickland on November 13, 1967, Kristen Heather Strickland was the oldest of two daughters. The family seemed relatively happy, and both children seemed well adjusted. By the time Gilbert was a pre-teen, the Stricklands had relocated from Fall River to Groton, Massachusetts, and appeared to be a normal family.

According to the Boston Globe, Gilbert was, at that time, a typical teenager – she earned pocket money by babysitting the neighbourhood kids, she loved soap operas, she took the bus to school and found her honours classes to be a breeze. A star student, Gilbert even joined the math club, and her date to the 1985 graduation prom at Groton-Dunstable Regional High School was the smartest boy in her class.

"She was not hotheaded or anything like that," remembered John Moore, who had lived next door to the Strickland family in the picturesque New England village. "She was a great kid – a cute kid. She seemed decent and normal, pretty intelligent, sharp."

The Moore and Strickland families were tucked away in a private area off Boston Road, and the two families initially began socializing together. Gilbert's father, Richard, worked as an electronics executive, and Claudia was a part time teacher and a full time homemaker. The families even became relatively close, with Gilbert often taking care of the Moores' two kids when they all came home from school, until their parents returned home after work.

However, the two families eventually had a falling out – a spat Moore was unwilling to explain in detail to reporters. The relationship fell apart, and one day, the Moores looked out the window to see a moving van parked in front of the Strickland family's small two storey home.

"Next thing we knew – boom – they're gone," Moore added.

Although Gilbert's early childhood indicated no significant issues, things began to change as she grew older. Friends recall that Gilbert became a skilled liar, and regularly boasted that she was somehow related to Lizzie Borden, a serial killer from the 1800s who had been accused of brutally murdering her father and stepmother with an axe.

In addition to habitually lying, friends claimed, Gilbert was frequently manipulative. She also had a tendency to threaten to kill herself whenever she was upset, and according to court records, would occasionally even make more violent threats.

Investigators later heard from ex-boyfriends, who described Gilbert as a skilled manipulator, who was "twisted, but not stupid." According to their accounts, Gilbert was capable of some dangerous, attention seeking behaviour – histrionics that included things like tampering with their vehicles or clawing their skin with her fingernails.

One of Gilbert's high school boyfriends even recalled an incident where an upset Gilbert had left a fake suicide note where he would find it, in which she claimed that she'd eaten glass.

Even Gilbert's father spoke about his daughter's habitual lying with his own psychiatrist. While Richard Strickland assured the doctor it wasn't true, he recounted how in college, Gilbert had managed to convince her roommates that her mother Claudia was an alcoholic who became abusive when she drank.

"She lied a lot," admitted Alberta Erickson, who had resided in Groton just across the street from the Strickland family. Her own daughter had been a close friend of Gilbert's when the girls were younger. "She had this blank stare, as if she was trying to make things up as she went along. She was one strange girl."

Erickson even recalled Gilbert's attempts to establish a familial link between herself and Lizzie Borden – Gilbert would often brag about this "distant, unsubstantiated" connection.

According to Erickson's daughter, Pamela Smethurst, Gilbert's constant lying was what eventually ended their friendship. The two girls rode the school bus together, and spent enough time together for Smethurst to pick up on when Gilbert wasn't being truthful.

Smethurst still vividly remembers, after searching high and low for a favorite shirt, she saw Gilbert wearing it soon after. According to Gilbert, the shirt belonged to her – but Smethurst recognized the well loved article of clothing immediately.

"We used to sit and watch 'General Hospital,'" Smethurst said, noting that the soap opera had been on in the afternoons when the girls came home from school. "And – this sounds freaky and almost made up, now. But there was this one character in the show who was this evil nurse. And I remember [Gilbert] said, 'I like Amy.' And I said, 'Oh, my God! Why would you like Amy?' And she said, 'I just like Amy.'"

Amy was "conniving and backstabbing," Smethurst added, and said she remembered thinking, "This is kind of strange."

A "highly skillful" nurse

After graduating from high school, Gilbert pursued a degree as a registered nurse at Greenfield Community College, which she completed in 1988. She studied both microbiology and surgical nursing, but made little impression on her instructors during her schooling.

"We certainly don't graduate anyone we don't feel comfortable with taking care of you, or I, or any of our patients," said Jean A.

Simmons, the coordinator of the nursing program at Greenfield Community College.

She also married Glenn Gilbert that same year, at the age of 21. The couple had met at Hampton Beach, New Hampshire, and had wed after a courtship of just three years. Glenn worked for a local optical lens firm, and they bought a home together in 1989 – after Gilbert was hired by the Veterans Administration Medical Center in Northampton, Massachusetts.

Located in the Leeds section of Northampton, the hospital is tucked away on more than 100 acres of pine forested land, known in the community as Bear Hill. The area has an established history – originally, the site housed the old Solomon Warner Tavern, a watering stop for the 19th century Boston-Albany stagecoaches.

The land was cleared in 1922, and it became the location of the VA's very first psychiatric hospital just two years later. The current 191 bed facility sprawls across 26 colonial buildings, separated by more than six miles of twisting roads, fountains, and shady trees.

Gilbert started working at the facility on March 6, 1989. She was stationed in the main medical unit, housed in Building One. She was a good nurse, according to her fellow workers – competent and very dedicated to the position. Even more than that, Gilbert was the kind of co-worker who went above and beyond for the other staff at the hospital. She remembered everyone's birthday, and was always the one in charge of organizing the facility's annual gift exchange during the holidays.

"At Christmas time, [Gilbert] always made sure that we had like a secret Santa," said a VA nurse named Karin Abderhalden, who had worked with Gilbert at the hospital.

Together, Gilbert and Abderhalden set up gift drives to donate items to families in need, and Gilbert ran the hospital's "Sunshine Fund," which would provide bouquets of flowers to new parents, newlyweds, or colleagues who had fallen ill.

On the C Ward, where Gilbert was stationed, she was known as a social butterfly. But in addition to being both pretty and popular, Gilbert was a "highly skillful" nurse, according to her superiors – particularly when it came to emergency situations, where Gilbert's cool head and calm reactions made her a favorite among the doctors.

"She readily recognizes actual or potential changes in patients' conditions," read one of the proficiency reports filed about Gilbert. "She is highly skillful in medical emergencies. And she is calm and compassionate with the mentally compromised patient. She is routinely assigned to ICU."

And according to clinical nursing coordinator Bernard P. LaFlam, her supervisors at the VA "had no problems with her nursing skills."

Gilbert and her husband welcomed their first child to the family in late 1990 – a baby boy. When Gilbert returned from her medical leave, however, she didn't come back to work the same shift she'd worked previously. Instead, she switched to the 4 p.m. to midnight shift – and shortly after, odd things began taking place during the evening hours.

The medical center's death rate quickly grew to three times what it had been in the previous three years, because patients were constantly dying during Gilbert's shifts. But as each incident took place, Gilbert's competency as a nurse shone through, and the other evening shift staff admired her ability to handle herself in a crisis.

In 1993, Gilbert gave birth to a second child – but her marriage to Glenn Gilbert had already become fairly strained. She'd been spending an awful lot of time with a co-worker, James Perrault, who was a security guard at the medical facility. An Army veteran of the Persian Gulf War, Perrault had left a position as a security guard at a local department store to join the VA hospital's police force, which boasted eleven members.

"We enjoyed each other's company."

He started working at the hospital just six months after Gilbert switched to the evening shift. Although he was only making $5,000 a year more than he'd earned hunting down shoplifters at the mall, the job at the VA was closer to what Perrault was ultimately hoping to achieve – legitimate police work.

While Perrault was on duty, VA policy dictated that he be required to respond to all cardiac emergencies, or "codes." When he wasn't dealing with codes or patrolling the roadways of the expansive hospital facility, however, Perrault was flirting with an attractive nurse who worked on Ward C – a nurse who seemed to always be involved whenever patients on the second floor medical unit of Building One faced cardiac arrest.

"During my rounds doing security, I stopped on the wards and I would talk to staff members," Perrault said. "And [Gilbert] and I seemed to have more in common, and we talked a lot."

When their shift ended at midnight, Gilbert would frequently go out socializing with Perrault and other hospital employees, instead of returning home to her husband and young children. They went to the VFW for beers – the Michael F. Curtain Post 8006 of the Veterans of Foreign Wars was only a mile away from the hospital's front doors.

Hidden away in the back of an old church, the large barroom offered $1.50 draft beers, a big screen TV, and a pool table. It was a great spot to unwind after work, and Perrault said Gilbert had hinted to him that her marriage had become increasingly rocky. When they emailed, Perrault said, she was seductive and funny, and soon, the conversations became sexually suggestive.

"After a few weeks of just flirting back and forth, we were down at the VFW, and after the VFW closed, I walked her out to her vehicle and we had a kiss," Perrault recalled.

By the end of the next year, Gilbert and Perrault had taken their relationship to the next level, and had begun a passionate extramarital affair. Gilbert's husband, Glenn, had met Perrault just once, on a summer boating excursion. But for some reason, as Gilbert's affair grew more serious, she started spending more time preparing home cooked meals for her husband.

And then, he noticed that his suppers didn't taste right.

"He told one witness that it was her goal to have her husband out of the house by Thanksgiving," prosecutors explained during a pretrial motion.

According to the prosecution, Gilbert had started lacing her husband's food with trace amounts of diuretics – a drug that would have been easy for her to obtain at work. Diuretics help to increase the body's discharge of urine, but Glenn Gilbert became violently ill on the evening of November 5, 1995.

After Gilbert drove her sick husband to the emergency room and he was examined by doctors, it was confirmed that he was suffering from low potassium and glucose levels. He was treated at the facility and then sent home.

But he got sick again just a week later. While Gilbert argues the incident was simply a harmless fainting spell as she'd been attempting to care for her husband, prosecutors claim it was an attempted murder.

Glenn's account of that day began when his wife had come home on her dinner break that evening. She told Glenn that she wasn't satisfied with the care he'd received at the local civilian hospital they'd visited, and that she wanted to draw a blood sample on her own to have it tested at the VA hospital, instead.

In the bathroom, Gilbert took two syringes from a canvas bag she'd brought home with her. In one of the syringes, Glenn saw a clear, odorless liquid – Gilbert assured him it was just a saline solution. She told him she was going to use it to flush his vein before she started drawing blood, a non-standard procedure which can potentially be dangerous.

She wrapped a tourniquet around his arm and inserted the needle. According to Glenn's account, "once the needle went in, his arm grew cold." The color began to drain from his chest and down his arms, and he said he attempted to pull himself away from his wife and asked her to please take the needle out. Instead, however, prosecutors said Glenn's testimony would be that Gilbert then "pinned him against the wall with her hip" and proceeded with the injection.

Then, Glenn said, he felt himself losing consciousness and slid down the wall to the bathroom floor.

Moments later, however, he awoke to see his wife – appearing flustered – shoving the syringes back into the canvas bag. He said Gilbert told him he'd just fainted at the sight of the needle, and added, "this was not going to work."

To Glenn, the incident was insignificant enough that he never even thought to tell the police. It was only brought up months later, during a custody dispute after Gilbert had made the decision to leave her family. But according to the authorities, the incident seemed to indicate that Gilbert may have been considering the possibility of murdering her husband.

"If it were the defendant's intent to kill her husband, one would have to wonder why she did not complete the act after he had slumped helplessly to the floor," Gilbert's defense team argued in a court brief.

While Glenn struggled to understand what had happened on the bathroom floor, and what his wife might be doing to his meals, Gilbert and Perrault were considering their options for the next step in their affair.

Although she'd offered up no proof, Gilbert had told Perrault that her husband had become abusive – and Perrault had reached the end of his rope.

"We had been at the Holyoke Mall, having breakfast, and during breakfast, I explained to her that because her husband had been abusing her, as she alleged, that if she did not leave him, I would leave her," Perrault admitted.

Immediately, he said, Gilbert burst into tears, but then walked over to the nearest pay phone and placed a call to Glenn. Perrault said he was close enough to hear Gilbert tell him that she was leaving him.

Glenn said he was trying to do what he could "to save the marriage, at that time." However, he wasn't a fan of his wife's new friend – "I disliked [Perrault's] character."

Within a week, Gilbert had moved out of the family's home, leaving the kids to live with their father. She found a small apartment in Easthampton, just a few blocks away from where Perrault lived. He helped her settle into her new apartment, and she rewarded him with his own key.

"We enjoyed each other's company," Perrault confessed.

From shift to shift

Gilbert continued to work at the hospital – but the deaths that seemed to occur all too often during Gilbert's shifts had aroused the suspicions of her co-workers. According to Frank Bertrand, a VA nurse who had resuscitated one of the elderly patients Gilbert had allegedly tried to kill, it almost seemed like she was two people at once.

"Things with [Gilbert] weren't always the way they seemed," he said. "I don't know if she had two personalities or something that she could turn on or turn off, much like an actor playing a role."

According to assistant US attorney William M. Welch II, when Gilbert started working the evening shift in the later part of 1991, the death rate on that shift tripled – while the death rate on the overnight shift, which she had stopped working in 1990, dropped back to the level it had been in 1988, before Gilbert accepted the $40,000 a year position with the VA.

"So, in essence, deaths followed Gilbert as she switched from shift to shift to shift," said Welch during a hearing ahead of Gilbert's trial.

But Gilbert's lawyer, Harry L. Miles, said the statistics indicating the rise in the hospital's mortality rate were "misleading."

"The problem with [that] evidence is that it tells you that an extremely skillful, extremely conscientious nurse can be singled out as having killed people because she acted conscientiously and competently," he argued at a hearing.

While many of the patients who passed away were elderly or already experiencing failing health, others were somewhat difficult to explain. Despite having no prior history of heart problems, patients were dying of cardiac arrest.

And, hospital workers had noticed, they always seemed to be low on ephedrine – a drug that, administered incorrectly, had the potential to cause heart failure.

Over the span of a few months, in late 1995 and early 1996, four of Gilbert's patients died. The cause of death was listed as cardiac arrest – and in each of the four cases, the suspected reason for the heart failure was an overdose of ephedrine. Once several of Gilbert's co-workers raised concerns about her possible involvement in the deaths, an investigation was launched at the hospital.

Gilbert resigned from her position shortly after, claiming she'd sustained injuries while on the job and needed time off to recover.

The relationship between Gilbert and Perrault also began to crumble, in the summer of 1996. That September, during the federal investigation into the high death rate at the VA hospital, authorities brought Perrault in for questioning.

And then, the bomb threats started.

While working at the hospital on September 26, Perrault answered a call from someone who claimed that they'd planted three bombs within the facility. The police were called down to the hospital, and patients were carefully evacuated from the building, but a search of the facility revealed that no explosives had been hidden inside.

A similar threat was made the following day, and again on September 30th – all while Perrault was working. It didn't take long for police to link Gilbert to the series of calls. In January of 1998, she was tried and convicted of making bomb threats, and received a sentence of 15 months in prison.

Federal investigators, though, weren't satisfied. They were compiling evidence to build a case against Gilbert, for her involvement with the increased cardiac deaths at the VA facility. By November of that year, Gilbert faced a new trial – for the killing of Henry Hudon, Kenneth Cutting, and Edward Skwira.

She was also charged with attempted murder in two other cases, the deaths of Thomas Callahan and Angelo Vella, and by May of 1999, she'd been charged again, in the death of a patient named Stanley Jagodowski.

"Just after leaving, one of the nurses saw Gilbert go into Jagodowski's room with a needle and a swab in her hand, under the pretext of 'flushing' his intravenous line with 'saline' to keep the line open," read court papers by Assistant US Attorneys William M. Welch II and Ariane D. Vuono.

However, Jagodowski hadn't been prescribed any injections – all of his medications were administered orally.

"[Gilbert] and Jagodowski were in the room alone when the [other] nurse heard Jagodowski yell, 'Ow, it hurts! You're killing me!'" prosecutors claimed. "As the nurse turned towards Jagodowski's room, she observed [Gilbert] exit."

Just a few minutes later, Jagodowski had suffered cardiac arrest – and within the next three hours, he would be dead. According to prosectors, his death was caused by Gilbert, who had used a heart stimulant – epinephrine – to push him into heart failure.

Doing it for the attention

During the November 2000 trial, prosecutors theorized that Gilbert had committed the murders in an attempt to spend more time with Perrault – she craved attention, they said. Of the 350 recorded patient deaths over the seven years Gilbert spent working at the hospital, she was on duty for more than half of them.

"The chance of that being a coincidence, [prosecutors] calculate, is 1 in 100 million," stated a Boston Globe article from October 8, 2000.

Prosecutors allege that Gilbert injected her patients with synthetic adrenaline, which "converted their hearts into fatally revved up and out of control pumps," according to the Boston Globe. It was an opportunity for Gilbert to show off for Perrault, they claimed.

"She liked the attention it brought," said Welch.

Welch added the prosecution intended to seek the death penalty, if the jury found Gilbert guilty of capital murder. The prospect "horrifies" the former nurse, according to the Boston Globe. Having already endured two and a half years in jail by the time the case went to trial, Gilbert was a shadow of her past self – her "fashionable blonde hair," attractive appearance, and glowing complexion had withered away, leaving her pallid, overweight, and mousy haired.

Still, she claims, she's no killer. Defense lawyers continued to argue that the patients had all died of natural causes, and claimed Gilbert was completely innocent.

"It's an unimaginable strain to be on trial for first degree murder, let alone looking at the death penalty," said David P. Hoose, Gilbert's defense attorney. "She has been absolutely adamant that she has done nothing wrong to any patient at the VA."

Her patients were all old, Gilbert argued. They had weak hearts, and were already sick. Some of them had even been diagnosed with terminal diseases. Her needles were used, according to Gilbert, to "comfort and heal." Not to inflict pain or damage.

"All of the people who died, died of natural causes. It's up to [the prosecution] to prove, beyond a reasonable doubt, some unnatural cause," said Gilbert's other court-appointed attorney, Harry L. Miles. "And we're saying they can't do it. There's certainly no eye witness saying that they saw her inject anybody with a substance. And there's no outright confession."

Even her co-workers had a difficult time accepting the idea that someone they had spent so many hours with could be capable of something so evil.

"Imagine having to testify against somebody who you worked closely with for a number of years on a matter like this – someone you liked and got to know and got to know their husband and their kids," said nurse Bertrand. "It bothers some people quite a bit. Who would ever suspect something like this?"

Jurors returned with a verdict on March 14, 2001. In three of the four cases, the jury determined Gilbert was guilty of first degree murder, and in the fourth, she was found guilty of second degree murder. She also received convictions for the attempted murders of the two other patients, and was sentenced to four consecutive terms of life in prison.

While Gilbert had initially attempted to appeal the sentence, she dropped the application in 2003. She remains behind bars in a federal prison in Texas.

JANE TOPPAN

AMY DEMPSEY

Jane Toppan

In 1887, a woman named Amelia Phinney was recovering from surgery for a uterine ulcer at Cambridge Hospital, Boston. Suffering pain from the procedure, she asked her nurse for something to ease the discomfort. The nurse, Jane Toppan, obliged, and although the medicine she gave to Amelia tasted foul, Jane encouraged her to finish it. As she drifted in and out of consciousness, she felt someone in the bed with her, kissing her face and caressing her. The attention suddenly stopped, and the following morning Amelia awoke and put the memories down to a strange dream. It wasn't until 1901, when Jane Toppan was arrested, that Amelia realised she had escaped the Angel of Death.

Her Early Years

Jane Toppan was born in Boston, Massachusetts, in 1857. Records about her early life are few and far between, but it is known that she was born Honora Kelley, the youngest of three daughters [2] (although some records show two daughters, and others suggest four) to Irish immigrants, Peter and Bridget Kelley. Bridget died of consumption (tuberculosis) when Honora was small, and Peter was left to raise his daughters alone. However, Peter was a chronic drunk. Known locally as 'Kelley the crack' (crackpot) for his eccentric and erratic drunken behaviour, [3] he was unable to cope with his daughters and in 1863 Peter placed his two youngest daughters, Honora and Delia, into the Boston Female Asylum, [4] an orphanage for orphans and destitute girls in Boston. [5]

When staff at the orphanage saw the poor state of the girls, they agreed to take them in. Peter Kelley later succumbed to insanity and was institutionalised for, allegedly, sewing his own eyelids together whilst working as a tailor. An older daughter, Nellie, was also reportedly institutionalised when she went violently insane in her twenties. [6]

The Toppans

In 1865, when Honora was only 7 or 8, she was taken in by the Toppan family as an indentured servant, meaning that she worked in service in return for bed, board, education and an agreed sum to be paid at the age of 18 when she would be released from her contract.

Although the family never formally adopted Honora, she took their last name and changed her first name to Jane. [8]

Jane excelled at school. She was described as 'brilliant and aggressive, and a leader of her class. She was also troubled, resorting to petty theft and lying. [9]

Jane's foster sister, Elizabeth, always treated her with kindness, but despite this, Jane's time with the Toppan family was not happy. Ann Toppan, the head of the household, treated Jane with disdain and made her feel ashamed of her Irish heritage. So much so, in fact, that she told friends that the young girl was an Italian immigrant whom the family had rescued from the streets.

Jane herself adopted this attitude, and in a bid to forget her own roots she would often be heard making disparaging remarks about other Irish people.

Ann Toppan was a cruel taskmaster and took every given opportunity to make her foster daughter feel small. As a result, Jane developed a personality which made her appear affable to others and was well-known for telling tall stories. But even this was ammunition for Mrs Toppan, as she attributed Jane's fondness for story-telling to the 'gift of the gab' – a talent for which the Irish were well-known. [10]

Despite Elizabeth's kindness, however, Jane developed an intense jealousy of her foster sister. Elizabeth was older by some years, and far prettier than 'plain Jane' and the younger girl envied Elizabeth's beauty and certain marriage.

These feelings were further compounded when, according to some reports, Jane was courted by a young man, an office worker from Lowell, when she was in her late teens. The relationship seemed to be going well when the young suitor gave Jane an engagement ring engraved with the image of a bird. Things turned sour, however, when the young man took a job in another town and fell in love with the daughter of his new landlord, and he called off the engagement. [11]

This betrayal proved to be a pivotal point in Jane's future behaviour, as she has been cited as saying *"If I had been a married woman, I probably would not have killed all of those people. I would have had my husband, my children and my home to take up my mind."* [12] Such was Jane's misery at being jilted, she began eating for comfort and gained a considerable amount of weight – at one point reaching 170lbs, which, on a diminutive 5'3" frame, is a lot of weight to carry. Her feelings of worthlessness grew, along with her resentment of the much-courted Elizabeth.

In 1874, Jane, by now 18, was released from her indenture and paid a lump sum of $50 (roughly $1064. 73 in today's money [13]) as per the terms of her contract. However, she decided to remain at the house in service to the family. Elizabeth married a young deacon of the local church, Oramel Brigham, and shortly afterwards her mother, Ann Toppan died, leaving everything to Elizabeth and nothing to her foster daughter, [14] a fact which further cemented Jane's resentment and loathing of her foster sister.

Jane stayed at the Toppan's house for a further ten years after she was released from her indenture. She was 28 when she eventually left in 1885. Although nothing is known about the circumstances of her departure – whether she was told to leave or left of her own free will – it *is* known that the ever gracious Elizabeth told Jane that there would always be a room at the house for her, should she wish to return. [14]

Nurse Jane

When Jane left the Brigham household, she decided to go into nursing, (one of only a handful of professions available to someone of Jane's social standing and gender), and began training at Cambridge Hospital in Boston.

Nurse Jane was a firm favorite among the patients – they loved her and nicknamed her 'Jolly Jane'. Her once maligned 'gift of the gab' stood her in good stead with the patients, who found her to be warm, attentive and caring.

Her co-workers, however, saw a vastly different side to their new colleague. She quickly became known as a liar and was wont to spread rumours about her colleagues and speak ill of people behind their backs to others. The rest of the staff quickly learnt not to trust the new trainee nurse.

Her professional ethics were also called into question when she was accused of stealing, and of altering patients' charts. Of course, Jane vehemently denied these accusations, and with no proof was allowed to continue with her training. [15] In actual fact, according to some sources, Jane's behaviour towards her fellow nurses, on occasion, led to a dismissal, and far from being dismayed that her antics had caused a colleague to lose her job, Jane would exhibit such extreme pleasure at their fate that it would alarm her fellow co-workers. [16]

The Angel of Death Emerges

It was during this time at Cambridge Hospital, that Jane began experimenting with her patients. At first, she would simply tamper with the patients' charts, or administer small amounts of medicine to the ones she liked to make them sick and prolong their stay. [17] However, as time went on this didn't appear to satisfy Jane's appetite for experimentation, and she began using her patients as guinea pigs in earnest, with deadly results. The small amounts of medicine used to induce sickness were no longer enough, and Jolly Jane turned to the drugs which were to become her hallmark – morphine and atropine.

To the Brink of Death

It is believed that in the beginning at least, Jane relied solely on morphine in her experiments. She would inject her chosen patient with the drug and stand back to watch the effects. The patient's pupils would contract, their skin would become clammy, and their breathing became laborious and loud. Depending on the dosage given, some of those patients would then slip into a coma, or even just stop breathing. Most satisfying to Jane, however, was when the patient would convulse, their body contorted with pain before they died.

On more than one occasion, Jane would take her patient to the brink of death before reviving them again, gaining a sense of professional pride in her life-saving skills. However, no matter how elated she felt having saved one of her victims' lives, nothing could compare to the thrill of seeing and feeling the life slip out of her target's body.

Soon, though, Jane had to add another ingredient to her deadly arsenal – atropine. Atropine is a fatal poison, derived from the belladonna plant, and was widely used in Victorian hospitals as a painkiller, as well as a go-to drug for many other conditions, such as whooping cough and tetanus. By introducing atropine to the mix, Jane could now witness (and enjoy) an entirely new set of effects. Pupils would dilate (rather than contract, as with the morphine), and patients would lose control of their muscles, often appearing intoxicated. The results would have been spectacular and gratifying for Jane to watch – her victims would sometimes laugh maniacally, or make low groaning sounds, much like that of a wounded animal. But possibly the most satisfying and exciting manifestation for Jane would be that of her patients pulling and plucking at objects around them, whether real or otherwise. Clothing, bed covers, their own fingers and toes – they would be compelled to pick continuously, even in their final moments, right up until death.

Jane was not content with merely administering the two drugs, though. She took great pleasure and interest in varying the dosages, watching the effects of the combinations. Her usual *modus operandi* seemed to be first injecting the patient with morphine and then, as they were about to lose consciousness, would offer them a glass of water with atropine dissolved in it. Sometimes, it seems, she would wait until the patient was near death from the morphine overdose, and then administer the atropine directly into the bowel by way of an enema, thus removing the last vestiges of dignity the patient might have left.

It is worth noting that Jane knew exactly what she was doing when using these drugs. Training of a nurse at that time was rigorous, to say the least. Much of it would have been what she had been used to in her years of service to the Toppans – cleaning, dusting, scrubbing floors and general 'housekeeping' of the wards for very little money, approximately $7 per month, out of which she had to buy all her books, as well as clothes and anything else she needed. But the training also included a weekly lecture on the medical profession and would have included the correct dosage and administration of drugs, of which morphine and atropine were just two. In fact, her final exam would have included questions on the correct dosage of atropine, morphine, and what should be done if a patient overdoses.

Jolly Jane Toppan knew exactly what she was doing.

There was more than one reason for Jane to use both atropine and morphine on her victims. Her first motivation was her own amusement. Jane got a huge thrill from watching her patients' reactions. She had a sadistic lust for their suffering and gained great pleasure from watching them writhe in pain before dying.

Her other reason for using the two drugs, however, was self-preservation. By using two substances which produced diametrically opposed reactions (morphine constricts the pupils, while atropine dilates them, for example), she could confuse the doctors who would examine the patients. In the absence of any textbook symptoms, the doctors would often attribute their deaths to a heart attack or diabetes. Jane would have derived a great deal of satisfaction from not only playing God with her patients but also from confounding the doctors. [18]

Sexual Thrill

Jane's perversion didn't stop at merely watching her patients suffer and die. Whilst it is not clear whether she sexually abused her victims, she later readily admitted to experiencing a sexual thrill from watching her patients dying, and this is borne out in the fact that she would climb into bed with them when they were close to death, pull them into her arms and hold them tight as the life drained out of their bodies. [19]

It was during this time that 36-year-old Amelia Phinney had her own brush with death at the hands of Nurse Jane. Amelia had had surgery for a uterine ulcer, a procedure which involved burning the ulcer with silver nitrate, and was recovering in bed at Cambridge Hospital. The post-operative pain she was experiencing made sleep impossible, and she became aware of someone standing by her bed. In the low light of the oil lamp, Amelia Phinney recognised her nurse, Jane Toppan, whose face, she recalled, had a look of deep intensity. Amelia asked Jane to fetch a doctor, as her pain was so bad, but Jane told her there was no need for a doctor, and she gave Amelia a drink, holding her up so she could sip.

Amelia did as her nurse told her, and shortly afterwards began to lose consciousness, but she later recalled that, through the haze, she felt the bedclothes being pulled back and another body joining her in bed. That body belonged to Jane Toppan, who proceeded to whisper to Amelia that everything would be alright. Amelia was powerless to move as the nurse caressed her, kissed her face, and peered excitedly into her eyes. The glass was once again brought to Amelia's lips as the nurse gently told her to drink some more, but the patient resisted and Jane suddenly left the bed and hurried from the room as though someone had disturbed her.

The next morning, when Amelia awoke, she put the bizarre happenings from the previous night down to a dream. [20]

Moving On

Although Jane was not liked by her colleagues, she had earnt the respect of some of the doctors at Cambridge Hospital, and, in order for Jane to further her studies, in 1888, they recommended her to the Massachusetts General Hospital.

Once again, Jane proved unpopular with her fellow nurses, who accused her of giving incorrect dosages to her patients. Talk was rife, with suspicions that several patients under Jane's care had died needlessly. However, it wasn't until the summer of 1890 that Jane was fired from her post at Massachusetts General, for leaving the ward without permission - a firm rule at the time.

Jane briefly returned to her job at Cambridge Hospital, but that was short lived as she was asked to leave because of reckless administration of opiates, a reputation which had dogged her career.

Private Nurse

In the summer of 1891, Jane decided to become a private nurse, and indeed she earned a reputation as the most successful private nurse in Cambridge. Her personality was not above reproach, however – her habit of telling lies and stealing continued and caused concern among some of her employers. Her free time did nothing to quash this reputation as Jane was known for drinking, and spreading rumours in her free time.

The Murders

Jane didn't need sick patients to murder, far from it. In fact, anyone who got in the way of what she wanted fell prey to the Angel of Death.

In 1895 Jane poisoned and killed Israel Dunham, her 77-year-old landlord because he was, according to her, feeble. Again, due to the complexities of her methods, doctors attributed his death to heart failure. Jane remained at no 19, Wendell Street, Boston, with Israel's widow, Lovey. However, by 1897 Jane had grown tired of her 'old and cranky' landlady. When the old lady fell ill in September of that year,

Jane 'nursed' her, with her standard morphine and atropine. Lovey Dunham died.

1899 saw Jane claim two more victims. In the summer of that year, Jane stayed (as she had for several years) at a rented vacation home in Cataumet, Cape Cod. She had maintained a somewhat strained relationship (at least on her part) with her foster sister, Elizabeth Brigham, and that summer Jane invited Elizabeth to join her at the house. The pair had enjoyed a pleasant picnic, and on return to the house, Jane exacted her revenge. She mixed morphine with mineral water and gave it to her foster sister. However, Jane wanted Elizabeth, the foster sister she had resented for so many years, to suffer...a fact borne out years later when Jane confessed to her crimes, stating that Elizabeth was "really the first of my victims that I actually hated and poisoned with vindictive purpose." A quick death was not revenge enough for Jane, so she dragged the death out until finally, Jane climbed into bed with and held the dying woman as she took her last breath, later saying "I held her in my arms and watched with delight as she gasped her life out."

In December of that same year, a 70-year-old widow named Mary McNear was suffering from a cold and cough, having picked it up on Christmas day whilst visiting her daughter in Cambridge, who wasn't very well herself. Mary's family were concerned about her health and raised the idea of hiring a nurse to care for the elderly lady. The family's doctor, Dr Walter Wesselhoeft, however, deemed it unnecessary, saying that she only had a cold and their servant could administer everything she needed for her recovery – bed rest and hot tea. The family still felt a nurse was needed and asked Dr Wesselhoeft to recommend someone.

That someone was Jane Toppan.

Cheered and encouraged by the care and attention the nurse was bestowing on her Grandmother, Evelyn Shaw (Mary's granddaughter) returned home happy, but Mary's coachman arrived shortly after to tell her that Mary had passed out and could not be revived. Evelyn returned to her grandmother's house. The Dr was already there when she arrived and told Evelyn that Mary had suffered a stroke after receiving her medication. Nurse Toppan had informed the staff but told them there was no cause for alarm. The cook, though, took it upon herself to send the coachman to Evelyn's house despite Jane's assurances that all was well. The following morning, December 29th, 1899, Mary McNear passed away without having regained consciousness.

After the funeral, Mary's relatives discovered that some of Mary's best clothes were missing, and voiced their concerns to the doctor that the nurse may have stolen them. He, however, was furious at the suggestion and the family dropped the matter. [21]

Nothing and nobody would stand in the way of Jane getting what she wanted. February 1900 saw Jane's victimology take a new twist- the murder of a friend. Myra Connors was an old friend of Jane's and worked at the Theological School as a dining matron. Jane needed money, so she poisoned Myra with strychnine and took her job. Her position was short-lived, however, when Jane's stealing came to light and she was dismissed.

The Ones That Got away

Jane's next three victims escaped death at Jane's hands, but this was by design, and not luck on their part. In 1901, at the age of 44, Jane took up residence with new landlords, Melvin and Eliza Beedle. Never one to enjoy paying rent, Jane poisoned her landlords, but only enough to make them sick enough to need the help of a nurse. As she nursed them back to health, Jane turned her attention to the Beedle's housekeeper, Mary Sullivan. Jane poisoned Mary so that she fell unconscious and Jane brought it to the Beedle's attention that their housekeeper was a drunk. She was fired, and Jane took over her job, living rent free. [22]

The Beginning of the End

Jane's downfall began in the summer of 1901. For many years she had rented a holiday home in Cataumet from the Davis family, who owned a hotel there. Jane had been lax in paying her rent, and although she was a favoured guest, the Davis' decided that it was time to call in Jane's debt of $500 (approx. $13,500 today). In June, Mattie Davis travelled to Cambridge to visit Jane at the Beedle's house and collect her back rent. Jane offered Mattie some mineral water, laced with morphine, and when Mattie became sick Jane gave her some more of the drug. Over the course of seven days, Mattie became sicker and sicker as Jane continued to poison her, even doing so under the watchful eye of a doctor until, on July 5th, Mattie fell into a coma and died. [23]

Jane accompanied Mattie's body back home and was there at the funeral. The family was grateful to the nurse for caring for Mattie, and a week later she moved into the Davis house to look after Mattie's widower, Alden, who was beside himself with grief at the loss of his wife.

Over the following weeks, Jane started no less than three fires in the Davis' house in an effort to kill the rest of the family, but each attempt was dealt with swiftly, much to Jane's disgust.

On July 26th, only three weeks after Mattie's death, Jane poisoned Genevieve Gordon, the Davis' youngest daughter. Jane told the family that Genevieve had committed suicide because she could not bear the grief of losing her mother. The death certificate stated that it was a heart attack.

Less than two weeks after the death of his daughter, Alden Davis also died at the hands of Jane Toppan, which the doctor put down to a cerebral hemorrhage.

Jane asked the oldest daughter of the Davis family, Minnie Gibbs, to write off the $500 debt she owed to the family. Minnie refused. [24] On August 12th, 1901, Jane murdered Minnie by way of morphine tablets. In a particularly twisted act, as Minnie lay dying Jane brought Minnie's ten-year-old son into her bed with her. There is no way of knowing whether any sexual assault took place on the boy. [25]

Having wiped out the entire Davis family, Jane returned to Lowell in late August. She had her sights set on marrying Oramel Brigham, her foster sister's widower. However, one person stood in her way – Oramel's sister, Edna Bannister, 77, so Jane did what she always did, and murdered her. She also poisoned Oramel himself, but only enough to make him sick so that she could prove her love for him by nursing him back to health. Nothing worked, and Oramel told Jane to leave, but not before Jane herself made a suicide attempt of her own.

Jane's Arrest

On August 31st, 1901, Captain Gibbs (Minnie Gibbs' father-in-law) ordered the bodies of the entire Davis family to be exhumed, to see whether his suspicions of their murders could be confirmed. By this time Jane had travelled to New Hampshire to stay with an old friend, Sarah Nichols, but had read about the exhumations in the newspaper.

On October 29th, 1901, Jane was arrested for the murder of Minnie Gibbs, and on December 6th, 1901, Jane was formally charged with four counts of murder – the entire Davis family.

Newspapers reported on March 31st, 1902, that Jane had undergone a psychiatric evaluation and had been classed as insane. She had admitted to the panel of experts that she had a sexual compulsion to kill, and confessed to 11 murders.

The Trial

The trial of Jane Toppan opened on June 23rd, 1902. The entire trial took less than eight hours, and the jury needed only 20 minutes to deliberate and deliver the verdict of Not Guilty by reason of insanity. She was sentenced to life at Taunton Insane Hospital, something she seemed delighted at. She believed that she would be freed in a matter of months because she would be able to convince the hospital that she was not, in fact, insane.

It later emerged that Jane had confessed to her defense lawyer, James Stuart Murphy, that she had committed more than 31 murders.

This confession was published in the New York Journal, including her admission that she had duped the panel into thinking she was insane, and that she felt very smug indeed at having outsmarted the experts. She also described the 'exquisite pleasure' killing had given her, and the lack of remorse she felt at the murders.

Jane laid the blame for the murders on the fiancé who had jilted her when she was in her teens, claiming *"If I had been a married woman, I probably would not have killed all of those people. I would have had my husband, my children and my home to take up my mind."*

Despite her belief that she would be freed, Jane Toppan spent the rest of her life at the asylum. Had she been freed, her killing spree would no doubt have continued – she is reported to have said that her only ambition in life was *"to have killed more people...helpless people....than any other man or woman who ever lived."*

Jane died on August 17th, 1938, at the age of 81. During the first two years in the asylum, her mental health was scrutinised, with many people asking why she was there as she appeared totally sane. There then followed a slow decline into insanity, with Jane often seen soothing other patients, crying out that they were dying, and trying to administer imaginary doses. Ironically, she became convinced that she herself was being poisoned and would stop eating, resulting in a dramatic weight loss. In a letter written to one of her doctors, she made reference to the 'poisonings':

"Taunton Lunatic Hospital, July 1, 1904.——"Doctor Stedman: I wish to inform you that I am alive, in spite of the deleterious food which has been served me. Many efforts have been made to poison me – of that I am very sure. I am thin and very hungry all the time. Every nerve is calling for food. Why can't I have help? I ate a pint of ice cream and four oranges Saturday and Sunday. (Signed) JANE TOPPAN

"NORAH KELLEY." [27]

In the end, Jane Toppan's deeds came back to haunt her.

NATASHA CORNETT

TRISH SAMUELSON

Natasha Cornett was born January 26th, 1979 in Pikeville, Kentucky.

Pikeville is located in the foothills of the Appalachian mountains. It is a mining town with most of its inhabitants devoutly religious.

"It's very beautiful scenery to grow up in," Cornett said. "But it's a suffocating place to live."

Born poor, Natasha was the product of an affair between her mother Madonna Wallen and her biological father, a police officer named Roger Burgess.

Her mother then left her husband, Ed Wallen, and raised Natasha alone. They lived in a trailer in Pikeville, Kentucky.

"She had energy to burn," her mother said. "She liked to draw. To read. She liked dogs and babies."

SCHOOL LIFE

Natasha was a good student in elementary school, behaving well and getting good grades. She seemed to be on the right path until one morning she found her mother laying unconscious. Madonna Wallen had overdosed on prescription drugs.

"My momma is on the bed naked," Cornett recalled. "With a bottle of pills laying next to her. I didn't know she was dying. It messed with me."

Around this time, Cornett's life began a downward spiral. She began suffering from anorexia. Then drugs. Then she began engaging in acts of self-mutilation, cutting her arms to "relieve her pain."

"Natasha started to engage in those acts as a means of getting control," forensic psychologist Roberta Nixon said. "She can control her diet. She can control her anger, or so she thinks, by cutting herself. She can control how she feels by doing drugs. Having a dim-witted mother certainly didn't help things either."

At one point, Natasha had lost over thirty pounds because of her anorexia as well as having over seventy cuts on her arms.

"I started cutting because I started going through a rough time with my mom," Natasha said. "It was a release."

"I don't know where that pain comes from," Natasha's mother, Madonna Wallen said. "She just says she has to do it to take away her pain."

In later court testimony, however, Wallen would admit to a history of physical abuse with her daughter.

"I used a belt one time and the buckles slipped from my hand," Wallen said. "And it hit her on the back of the leg. But it made a bruise on her."

Wallen later said that there was sexual abuse of Natasha by her husband whom she originally believed to be Natasha's father.

"Natasha had a really bad upbringing," C. Berkeley Bell, the District Attorney General for Tennessee said. "Lot of hard times. She came from a very dysfunctional family. Hard time in school. Was an outcast. Was ostracized by her classmates."

HIGH SCHOOL DROPOUT

Natasha entered high school but dropped out before her freshman year was complete. Her best friend was Karen Howell who would later be part of the "Wild Bunch" that Cornett would lead on a killing spree.

"Karen was my life raft," Natasha said. "She was the only person that understood me and let me be me. She knew my pain. She went through the same stuff."

Like Natasha, Karen had a dysfunctional family. Her father was an abusive alcoholic and her mother had a nervous breakdown. She came from a strict, religious family with her mother forcing her to stand on a Bible when she misbehaved. She was also bipolar.

"They were like two peas in a pod," Nixon said. "But in court interviews Natasha seems to more of a realization of what took place that night. Karen remained a petulant teenager, sullen and angry. Natasha was the better talker of the two so Karen followed her lead.

BIPOLAR DISORDER

Natasha was eventually diagnosed with bipolar disorder and in one episode had to be hospitalized at the Ridge Treatment Center in

Lexington, KY. She had to leave the hospital after eleven days, however, as that was all the time the state health benefits would allow.

"Bipolar disease is brutal and even more so for people in low income circumstances," Nixon said. "It is extremely hard to treat. The amazing thing here is that she was only hospitalized for eleven days. After that, she doesn't appear to have gone through any kind of outpatient treatment program aside from an aborted session with a counselor. With people like Natasha, they need medication to keep their anxiety and impulses under control. Without it, anything can happen and anything will happen."

Natasha's mother began to see the rapid decline in her emotional state. Her choice of clothing would be reflect her mood and growing anger.

"From the seventh grade," Wallen said. "She just started changing. The big baggy pants. The rope with the emblems hanging. Everybody thought it was weird."

"I started drinking and smoking and associating with people that were weird," Natasha said. "You don't have to be perfect around them."

Natasha sought acceptance and eventually found it in the Goth subculture. Still, with the rapid mood shifts and change in dress, Natasha's own mother insists that there are three versions of Natasha.

"There is the sweet, caring girl," Wallen said. "There is the girl who would do anything for her friends, and there is a dark side that likes to play on a Oujia board, do seances and play vampire games."

MARRIAGE

At the age of seventeen, Natasha married Stephen Cornett. It was no ordinary ceremony, however. The bride and groom wore black and dog collars.

"We'd been friends for awhile," Natasha said. "It seemed like the logical thing to do."

The union only lasted a couple of months. Steven left without warning, abandoning Natasha. The dissolution of the marriage caused Natasha to spiral further into depression.

"It was awful," Natasha said. "I just kinda caved in on myself."

Natasha then fully immersed herself in the Goth subculture even further. She donned black clothing and listened intently to the dark, depressing music. She would pierce her eyebrows and lips with safety pins as well as use black lipstick and nail polish.

"For most kids," Nixon said. "The Goth culture is a way to rebel. To control their own image. It is a relatively harmless phase for most involved. They're young. They act out. Then they grow out of it. For some kids, however, like Natasha, it is more than that. She's disturbed to begin with and wants to take it beyond the dark music and black get-ups and really wants to do harm to someone. She realized that the Goth culture was a way to make people afraid of her. This is how she would gain power. She could control people by being their 'darkness consultant.'"

NATASHA THE VAMPIRE

She became a self-described "vampire" and named her black dog "Malkavian" after the vampires in her favorite vampire fantasy board game as well as collecting all of Anne Rice's vampire novels.

"She was a dark soul who'd give you the willies," a local teen said in describing her.

Natasha covered the walls of her bedroom in her trailer with numerous dark messages including "I hate the world" as well as drawing inverted crosses.

"Tasha would start hearing voices," Wallen said. "Talking to people on the Oujia board. Her and Karen fed on each other. You know. It just kept getting worse. She wanted away from all the people that called her 'freak.'"

Her drug use and drinking increased but she was able to attract a group of friends, most of whom looked up to her. The group consisted of three girls. The petite Karen Howell and the overweight, awkward Crystal Sturgill.

Sturgill was molested by her step-father and had been kicked out of her home. She needed a place to stay and hooked up with Karen and Natasha.

The threesome would go around the sleepy Kentucky town, spray painting pentagrams, the satanic number 666 and inverted crosses across the walls of buildings and homes.

"They were all sort of drop outs," reporter Bill Jones said. "Who fell through the cracks in school. They dressed in Gothic fashion, black clothing. Black make-up. Looks Satanic, if you're looking for Satanic that's what might come to mind."

"Everything that we did," Natasha said. "Was very destructive but also self-destructive. Nothing was done to harm anybody but ourselves."

Natasha began spelling her name backwards, 'Ah-Satan', spray painting it across the walls of the town.

"She used the name to intimidate," Dixon said. "In an odd way, that was part of her charm. She was more 'out there' than the impressionable kids in her town. She held sway over Karen Howell and Crystal Sturgill, both of whom were looking for someone they could look up to. So while Natasha was an outcast at school she was able to assemble other outcasts and cast them under her spell. She became the devil of choice to worship."

The gang carried around two books with them, *The Book of Black Magic* and the *Complete Book of Magic and Witchcraft*. The three girls would go to motel rooms or Natasha's mother's trailer to hang out, drink alcohol and each other's blood. They would also engage in seances and Satanic rituals they would read about in books.

"When it comes to the occult," Dixon said. "Most young people just dabble around with it. In the case of Natasha and her gang, however, she led them over the edge. They were dumb kids out looking for kicks and she pushed them into something that they probably would not have gotten involved in had it not been for her own dark compulsions."

ROAD TRIP TO HELL

"We're going to start armageddon," Natasha informed one of her friends. "I hate, therefore I am" became her mantra.

Natasha and the "Wild Bunch" decided to go on a road trip to New Orleans. They were obsessed with the vampire books of Anne Rice and thought about the prospect of meeting her. Talks began and the entire group wanted to leave the small town of Pikeville behind.

"All I could think of was I need out," Natasha said. "I need out. I need out. I need out. I can't breathe, I need out."

The group of girls were now joined by some equally nefarious young men. The first is Joe Risner who is Karen's boyfriend and at twenty years old, the oldest in the group. Risner, never knew his own father and was known as the quiet, introverted type. He wanted to impressed Karen but was insecure as his love interest seemed more infatuated with Natasha then with him.

Edward Dean Mullins was nineteen and the only one from the group that comes from an intact family that goes to church. He is struggling with self-esteem issues, however, as women reject him until he meets Natasha. James Bryant is fourteen but seemingly the most volatile of the "Wild Bunch". His mother has abandoned him and left him alone with an alcoholic father. Natasha and Karen met him on a street corner and picked him up because they thought he looked "cool." Mostly likely, they saw him as someone the could use to do their dirty work.

"I had been friends with Joe for awhile," Natasha said. "Joe was dating Karen. Crystal needed a place to stay and she was friends with Dean (Mullins)."

Jason was the last entry into the "Wild Bunch." It was apparent, however, that he and Natasha didn't always see eye to eye. According to detectives, Jason was not as "controllable" as others in Natasha's group.

"Jason didn't make a huge impact on me," Natasha said. "He seemed dangerous. Like people pretend to be bad. I thought that was his hook. He was the 'bad boy.'"

Natasha's mother's trailer would be their primary hangout where they would drink, do drugs and later plot out their killing spree.

"Prior to leaving (for the road trip)," Bell said. "The defendants would watch 'Natural Born Killers.' That movie depicts individuals who are carefree, killing people. There don't appear to be from that movie, any consequences (to violence). They may have felt that there were not going to be any consequences for their actions. I really don't know what it takes for a group of people to take on that mentality of murder. They had no concept of tomorrow. Or consequences. And they just don't care."

The members of the gang become increasingly excited as they discuss the prospects of what will take place on their killing spree. Finally, they have some excitement in their boring, despondent lives with Natasha at the head.

"She seemed to be the leader of the group," Jones said. "And someone in the group said 'we're going to make headlines.'"

MOTEL SEVEN PIT STOP

The group piled into Risner's mother's car, a compact Chevy Citation. Before they would hit the highway, they rented out room number seven at the Colley Motel in Pikeville. Despite Natasha's apparent disdain for Jason, the young fourteen year old had cut Natasha's initials into his arm that night at the motel. The group then attempted to burn the satanic numbers 666 into the motel carpet with candle wax.

They would then begin their self-mutilation ritual.

"Me and Karen started cutting," Natasha said. "And at first, it was just to cut. Then I wanted to die. I thought eventually if I cut myself so many times I would just bleed out. Mostly it was just me and Karen drinking each others blood. We just didn't do seances."

Crystal maintains that they were not part of a vampire cult or nor did they worship Satan. "We dressed in black and we'd stand out. And we did self-multilation. We were the freaks, the outcasts."

"We were trying to find answers, " Crystal said during in interview with Campus Life. "We all had been to church. It didn't provide answers. We were interested in Wicca, books on witches and spells. We were anarchists."

"They wanted to go to New Orleans," Natasha said. "Because that was the only place I was familiar with. And I said I wouldn't go back down there without some kind of protection."

Natasha was referring to the fact that she claimed to be raped in New Orleans although no charges were filed.

The motel owner, Jim Cochran, said that he rented out the room to Risner and described him as "polite and courteous". Risner, who also wore the Goth black make-up was described by detectives as "lanky and long-haired." A week before their killing spree, Natasha was in a Pikeville grocery store where she led Risner around by a dog chain fastened to a collar around his neck.

The group started a fire in the motel room and they were worried the manager would call the cops.

"Karen had just gotten into trouble," Natasha said. "And she didn't want to go back to juvenile. Jason just got out of juvenile and he didn't want to go back. And I was ready to run away at any given moment so it just kinda came together. We were all going to run away."

The group then vandalized and burglarized other Colley Motel rooms during their stay. They stole a television set and several pairs of work boots.

ROUTE 666

The group of disaffected youth drove to Forty-Acre Field, a remote campground where other teens would hang out. They started a campfire then at some point that night or early in the morning they burglarized two homes in a town called Paintsville. It was there they stole two semi-automatic handguns.

They thought about performing a carjacking as Joe's mother's Chevy Citation kept overheating. Nonetheless, they went onto U.S. Highway 23 south into Virginia.

The group was ticketed for speeding in Gate City, Virginia on April 6th but were allowed to continue on.

"Based on the evidence of what their stated purpose was," Bell said. "The night before they left. They were preparing to leave Pikeville. Go across the country. Robbing and killing people."

The group then drove into a used car lot and tried unsuccessfully to hot wire a vehicle.

They kept driving and an hour later, they stopped at the Interstate Highway 81 rest stop in Greeneville, Tennessee.

"Karen needed to pee," Natasha said.

Tragedy would ensue as the group came upon the Lillelid family at a truck stop in Greeneville,

THE LILLELID FAMILY

Thirty-four year old Norwegian Vidar Lillelid, his twenty-eight year old wife Delfina, their six year old daughter Tabitha and two year old son Peter were having lunch on a park bench.

Vidar, who worked as a hotel bellman, had taken his family to a religious convention in Johnson City. They were on their way home to Nashville. He had been in the USA for ten years. His wife, Delfina was a native of New Jersey but had parents who had immigrated from Honduras. The two had married in 1989 and moved to Knoxville four years earlier from Miami because they wanted a nice place to raise their two children. The two were described as "devoutly faithful" and "humble" by those who knew them.

"The Jehovah's Witnesses were having a convention abut thirty miles north," Jones recalled. "They had been to that convention and they were going home. Jehovah Witnesses are known for being active in trying to recruit new members. They leave pamphlets and that sort of thing. That may have been the worst thing they could have done."

"I think they were doing a little proselytizing there," Bell said. "It was just part of their religion that they go out and try and talk to people. They saw the defendant's unusual appearance. They may have though that they needed some discussion about the Lord."

Vidar and Delfina approached the group and asked if they believed in God. Natasha spoke for the everyone, saying she dd not believe in God, as he had never come to her aid when she prayed as a child.

"The whole scenario just drips with tragic irony," Dixon said. "On one hand, we have the Lillelid family. They are sweet and naïve. They are following the dictates of their church to go out and invite as many members as they can for their church. Then there are these cult members who a diametrically opposed viewpoint. They have their own beliefs. Only theirs are something far more sinister."

KIDNAPPING AT GUNPOINT

According to Natasha, it was Joe who initiated the kidnapping of the family.

"It was when Joe said he wanted to converse with Vidar about his religious beliefs," Natasha said. "That just brought up red flags, because Joe was not a religious man. I tried to convince him (Joe) that we should just leave and get on our own way. Every step that he took, I was there trying to prevent it."

Natasha stated that it was never their intent to rob and kill the Lillelids. She became alarmed with Joe who went back to his car and got his gun. Then after conversing with Jason, Joe pulled the gun out on the Lillelids.

Detectives confirmed that Joe Risner admitted that he was the one that pulled the gun. Natasha remained steadfast in her own statement that she tried to stop Joe.

"He was like 'nothing is gonna happen'," Natasha said. "'We just need your car.' All I could do was just look at them and apologize."

Vidar immediately offered his keys and wallet, pleading for the killers to not harm his family.

"They put them in their respective cars and took off," Bell said. "They got off the Interstate. Just a few miles down the road."

"I didn't think that the people that I was around could actually do anything bad," Natasha said. "Even Jason. I thought I could stop something."

Detectives found out otherwise, however. During interviews with the other members of the group, they believed that Natasha was the instigator. She was the one that members of the group thought could "draw on demons" and was the driving force behind the robbery.

Joseph Risner forced the family into the Citation. They drove along until they reach a remote area.

"It's a dead end, gravel, one lane road," Jones said. "They go down the end of that road and force the people out of the car."

The family is terrified. Vidar continued to plead for mercy. Young Peter is clinging to his mother's leg, his arms wrapped tight around her waist.

"This group of very strange looking people is surrounding them and laughing," Bell said. "And they see the weapon."

"I can't imagine what that would have been like," Jones said. "To know that your family was in peril like that."

According to Natasha, it was Risner that pulled the gun on the family but now on the deserted road it was Jason Bryant, the fourteen year old, who held the family at gunpoint.

"All of a sudden Jason pulled the gun up," Natasha said. "All I could see was rage on his face. And Joe walked away from it. He was like, 'I can't do that.' And I was like 'Jason, what are you doing? And he just started cussing. 'Get the fuck outta the way! Get the fuck outta the way! Move! Unless you wanna die, move!

"I got in between Jason and the family to where the gun was pointed at me and tried to convince him to not do that. I begged and I pleaded for what seemed like an eternity for him to stop. When I discovered that there was no stopping him, I begged for at least the children to be saved. He told me that if I didn't move, he would shoot me."

"I don't think I would have moved anyway until he promised and swore to me that he would not harm the children. That's when I moved. I didn't think that I could do anything to prevent it if I was dead."

During the testimony, Natasha, Risner and Karen Howell said that Bryant did the shooting. Bryant, however, said that Risner and Edward Dean Mullins fired the shots and later forced him to take the blame.

Gunpowder was found on Mullins, however. The detectives and prosecuting attorney believed that the entire group somehow were involved in the shootings as over seventeen shots were fired.

"If you wanted to be a member of this group," Bell said. "You had to participate in this ritualistic killing."

"I don't know which (of the family) got shot first," Bell said. "But the rest of them are observing their family being shot."

"The indication was that the children were shot last," Jones said. "The little girl had apparently walked around in her mother's blood. The boy even though he was two years old was shot in the head."

"I didn't watch," Natasha claimed. "I sat in the back of the van and just screamed. Please don't hurt them. Please don't hurt them. Please don't hurt them. Jason said 'Stop fucking crying.' He just laughed."

Six year old Tabitha was shot in the head. Peter was being held by his mother as he was shot. Each of the victim was shot in the eye as a 'signature' move.

"The males were shot in the right eye," Bell said. "And the women on the left."

"It was a ritualized killing," Dixon said. "Call it bonding through murder. They would hoop and holler and cheer each other on. "

The group left Risner's mother's car at the scene as it became stuck in the mud. They stole the family's van, the youths took off in the hopes of going to Mexico.

But not before they had dragged the bodies over, lying the four bodies parallel to each other so it appeared like a four-pointed star.

Joe laughed as they drove over the bodies, hearing the crunch of bone under the weight of the van.

THE AFTERMATH

Vidar and Delfina were found dead, tire tracks across their clothing. Tabitha was still alive when found but died en route to the hospital. Two year old Peter was shot in the torso and the eye. Amazingly, the boy survived although he is now blind in one eye and permanently disabled.

"Peter survived," Jones said. "The two year old boy had been shot through the eye with the bullet exiting the side of his head. It didn't kill him. He's disabled by the extent of his injuries. He had difficulty walking and of course, blind in one eye.

The youths showed no remorse after the shooting. People who lived nearby heard gunshots, laughing and shouting as they left the family for dead. The police were called and the Sheriffs discovered the dead bodies of the Lillelid family.

ON THE RUN

"After you witness something that atrocious," Natasha said. "I didn't know what to do."

The group went on the run, altering their plans to go to New Orleans. Instead, they headed to Arizona/Mexico border.

Two days after the shootings, Natasha and her cohorts were arrested by US Customs and Immigration officials in Arizona.

"They had been down into Mexico," Bell said. "And as they were coming back through the computers at the border had not been functioning. So the border could not check on who was coming in and out. But just as that group came back in the computer suddenly started working. And when they put the license tag in the system they got a hit. And they were arrested there in Arizona."

The detectives and defense attorney who dealt with Natasha after the arrest vary widely from her own well-thought versions of what took place that night.

"She was a vampire who worshiped Satan," said an officer who spoke to Natasha after her arrest. "She was on the dark side. Very bitter towards everyone."

Natasha allegedly told her first defense attorney, Eric Conn, that she was 'Satan's Daughter.' The attorney decided to play up that aspect of her defense as he hoped to get her a lenient sentence if she was declared insane.

"After Eric Conn got up in the devil worship and vampirism," Wallen said. "It kept getting worse and worse."

Natasha blames her first lawyer, Conn, for her lackluster defense.

"I don't know why it was me that was picked out of everyone else," Natasha said. "I know he did a lot of damage to me and my case.

"I didn't tell him that I even had any inclination toward that," Natasha recalled. "I knew he was a lawyer wanting to represent me pro bono. At no point had I ever been a satanist. Ever. Once something like that is said. You can't just take it back."

Conn was later replaced by Stacy Street but the damage had been done.

Natasha's current court-appointed attorney stated that "he (Conn) volunteered to represent her, then immediately began negotiating movie rights.

SOUVENIRS OF A KILL

"Each one of these killers," Berkeley said. "Took an individual trophy from their victims. And kept it attached to a chain or a wallet."

Karen Howell took Vidar's social security card and Tabitha's 'Hello Kitty' merchandise. Natasha took Tabitha's social security card and her wallet. Sturgill had taken the keys to the Lillelid home all for souvenirs.

DEATH PENALTY?

"We were very concerned that the proof might focus on the juveniles as being the shooters," Bell said. "Juveniles can't get the death penalty. And if they can't get the death penalty we were concerned that no one else would get the death penalty either. What we reached was an agreement that we'd have a hearing."

A media circus followed the trial as an angry mob descended upon the teenagers as they entered the courtroom.

"Someone yelled that I was Charles Manson's daughter," recalled Sturgill.

In the trial, all six defendants had different stories as to how events took place that night and who pulled the trigger.

"It is my position that it was part of an initiation," Bell said. "That everybody had to participate in the shooting."

"Natasha clearly was the ring leader in all of the killings here," Dixon said. "She was the most articulate and confident of the group. The young men in the group were all shy types, eager from some female validation, with the possible exception of Jason who was a budding psychopath. But again, he was a dim-witted fourteen year old pitted against a smooth-talker in Natasha. Sturgill and Howell looked up to Natasha in their own ways as well. Sturgill was social awkward, overweight. She finally found people she could call friends and would do whatever they said. And Karen would not become violent on her own. These individuals were all like that, they could be violent but needed someone to light the fuse. And Natasha struck the match for everyone.

CONVICTION

Natasha was convicted on March 13th, 1998 with the five other youths. She reached a plea bargain where she plead guilty to all of the charges to avoid the death penalty.

In her court testimony, Natasha maintained that she was not the shooter of the four victims. She kept asserting that she tried to prevent the deaths of the Lillelid family members.

All of the defendants were sentenced to three life terms plus twenty-five years without the possibility of parole.

"She wasn't the shooter," Natasha's mother said, maintaining her daughter's innocence. "She got the same thing as the shooter."

PRISON LIFE

Natasha is housed at a prison in Nashville. She has earned her GED and her mother Madonna claims that her daughter serves as a "mentor to fellow inmates as they work to earn their GED."

"I was a teacher's aide for about a year," Natasha said during a newspaper interview.

Her troubled times continued, however, as on August of 24th 2001, she and death row inmate Christa Pike allegedly attacked a fellow prisoner named Patricia Jones.

They tried to strangle Jones to death with a shoe string after all three were placed in a holding cell with Natasha during a fire alarm.

Pike was on death row for torturing and beating a woman to death when they were Job Corps students in 1995.

Another inmate, the twenty-year old Jennifer Szostecki started the fire which created confusion during the fire alarm. This allowed Christa Pike to gain access to Patricia Jones.

Jones allegedly teased Pike about her upcoming execution.

"All she does is snitch on me and stab me in the back," Pike said during a phone call with her mother.

Natasha allegedly struggled with Jones before Pike came from behind and started to choke Jones with the shoe strings from a hiking boot. Natasha was Pike's friend and Szostecki's "girlfriend."

Letters filed in criminal court show Szostecki's obsession with Natasha.

"I love you," Sozstecki wrote. "I hate you. I miss you. I want you. I need you."

Pike was later charged with attempted murder while there was insufficient evidence to charge Natasha.

"I expected big women with shanks and stuff like that," Natasha said of her time in prison. "You know, like that typical prison scene that you would see in a movie. But it's not like that. You just get up, go to meals, have an hour out for recreational purposes and watch television and read."

PETER LILLELID

Peter Lillelid would be the subject of a custody battle between his USA based relatives and his aunt in Sweden. His aunt and uncle from Sweden won custody and Peter was sent to be in their care.

They kept him shielded from the media and he does not like to read the accounts of what happened to his parents and sister.

A MOTHER'S KILLER :

THE TRUE STORY OF NICOLE KASINSKAS

CHRISTINE GOODMAN

Nicole Kasinskas was a quiet, unassuming teenage girl. She was born and raised in Nashua, New Hampshire to Anthony Kasinskas and Jeanne Domenico.

"I lived with both of my parents and my younger brother until I was eleven years old," Nicole said. "And my parents divorced and my Dad moved out."

"I think after my parents got divorced and I was dealing with that, I became a little bit angrier. I had a little bit more resentment towards him, and it did change my perspectives about myself and about life in general, I guess even as an eleven year old."

In May of 2002, she found "romance" as a fifteen year old on-line with eighteen-year old Billy Sullivan.

Sullivan lived in a town called Willmantic where he worked as a line cook at McDonald's.

"Nicole hadn't had a lot of boyfriends," prosecuting attorney Kirsten Wilson said . "She was really caught up by the attention by this guy who was saying amazing things to her about how beautiful she was and what she meant to him."

They would communicate daily through e-mail, letters and phone calls. Despite not having met in person, they both declared love for each other within days, speaking of marriage and planning their future together.

"They filled in sort of the gaps of everyday communication and relationships with fantasies and making these assumptions on who the other person was," Wilson said.

"He lived in Connecticut and so our relationship was almost one hundred percent over the phone," Nicole said. "But it became everything to me very quickly because of the amount of attention that he paid me, and I didn't really feel that I was getting that from anywhere else."

Nicole had been vulnerable to Sullivan's Internet advances as she was a loner with very few friends in high school. She was routinely bullied at school by other girls. On one occasion, she was walking down the hall and one of her bullies had pulled her sweatpants down to her ankles. Nicole was not wearing any underwear, furthering the humiliation. Nicole refused to go back to school the next day after that incident.

"The bullying at school certainly made Nicole vulnerable to someone like Sullivan," forensic psychologist Fiona Russo said. "She's lonely, she's being picked on at school and completely humiliated. She stuck to herself and so when some guy pays attention to her, even when it is only online, her fantasy life goes into overdrive. She's able to project things on him that he doesn't deserve or merit."

The more severe the bullying became, the more Nicole began to withdraw and cling to Sullivan.

"As I got older, it was easier for me to isolate from people," Nicole said. "I think at that point I had just gotten used to being more alone as opposed to being around people. And it just became a part of who I was. Maybe if I was more open or maybe if someone had tried harder to reach out, that it could've been different."

Nicole's mom, Jeanne, was her best friend. Jeanne worked at an elementary school for a period of time, holding down such jobs as a crossing guard, a lunchroom monitor, and a paraprofessional for about three years before taking a job where she worked on group contracts for the Benefits, Brokers and Administration department.

"Jeanne Domenico was well loved in the community," Wilson said. "Hard worker. Really sort of a bright, energetic, sweet woman. She was trying to make her daughter happy."

Despite the bullying at school, Nicole got straight A's at school and made her mother happy whenever she made the honor roll.

"School really became my self-worth and I really identified with, like whatever my grades were," Nicole said. "However I was doing in school I felt it reflected on me personally, because I felt that it was so much a part of who I was. I never got in trouble in middle school. I never got spoken to. I never had a detention. It never really crossed my mind to do anything that would be against the rules."

"It would have been helpful if there was more of an acknowledgment that I was doing so well. I think it also would've been helpful if there was more involvement with guidance or something. Just more of a like a check-in...see how things are going."

"Somehow, someway, Nicole got lost in the cracks," Russo said. "That in no way justifies what she did. It may be how she justified it during this time. Her parents are divorced. She doesn't see her Dad. Her mom is working all the time. There had to have been days where she felt intense loneliness Going to school just to be ignored or bullied. To a fourteen year old girl you really may not see the light at the end of the tunnel. So you seek an outlet. Some turn to drugs. Nicole found her own drug in the form of the words that came out of Sullivan's keyboard."

MOTHER AND DAUGHTER TROUBLES

At least on the surface, there were no problems between mother and daughter.

Until Nicole ventured on-line and met Billy Sullivan.

Her mother found out about the relationship and wanting to make her daughter happy, drove the young teenager out to Connecticut so she could meet Sullivan for the first time.

"This was a two hour drive from Nashua to the place in Connecticut where Sullivan lived," Russo said. "It is easy to say here is where Jeanne made a fatal mistake. But in her mind, it is all innocent. Her daughter is fourteen and begging her to drive out to meet this guy. Begging and begging. Until she finally she relents."

More visits followed but friends and classmates knew little of the teen's relationship. Sullivan had informed some of his friends that he had a girlfriend that was "out of state." Other than that, he revealed very little about his personal life.

"He's quiet, he didn't really like to talk," recalled Danny Goss who was a classmate of Sullivan. "But he was good in school and didn't get in any trouble."

"I think the relationship intensified to a degree that Jeanne herself didn't anticipate," Russo said. "And it is easy to play Monday morning quarterback here but there had to have been some kind of father figure present to say 'hey, this is an eighteen-year old working at McDonald's. You are a fourteen year old honor student. You have a future. Don't blow it on this guy. But it isn't like teens listen to you anyway."

The two teenagers soon discussed the prospect of moving in together. Her mother quickly objected to this idea as well as nixing the idea of Nicole sharing a joint bank account with Sullivan.

But the young man later stayed overnight one weekend with Nicole's mother's full consent.

The relationship is the first for Nicole. She pedestalizes Sullivan as everything she has fantasized about is coming true.

"Nicole had a void in her life," Russo said. "When her parents divorced it certainly affected her psychologically in the way she viewed men. Then along comes Sullivan whose older and more experienced. She gets the love from him that perhaps she sought from her father. The older man, wiser than his years, showering her with attention. She was vulnerable to that."

"Her father didn't have too much to do with her after the divorce. She had that longing in her heart for that male figure. And along came Sullivan."

PERSONAL DEMONS OF HIS OWN

Sullivan, however, had his own personal demons he was fighting.

"He did have mental health issues," Wilson said. "He had been hospitalized a number of times. During high school he had some behavioral issues. Some anxiety, that kind of thing."

It was later revealed that Sullivan had been on numerous psychiatric medications to curb his depression, anger and schizophrenia. He had been weaning himself off the meds, however, and on one occasion he engaged in an argument with Nicole's mother over dinner.

Jeanne had asked Billy if she liked the dinner she had prepared. He said yes and then Jean made the comment that "I bet you don't get that too much at home."

Sullivan was highly defensive over anything that involved his home life. When Jeanne made that comment, he turned hostile.

"Sullivan was protective of his home life," Russo said. "If anyone insulted his mother or if he even perceives that someone is insulting his mother then he gets abusive. He did this to Jeanne, who had obviously made nothing more than an idle comment. That was the first warning sign and the relationship should have ended then and there."

Nicole, however, defended her young beau and from that moment the tug of war for her heart began.

"Nicole's own naivete comes to bore at this point," Russo said. "She has no experience with boys and here is this older guy that she looks up to, almost as a father figure of sorts, who turns her against her own family. Against the one person who loved her the most. Her mother. It is a tug of war that the mother loses simply because her daughter's hormones are raging and she doesn't yet have the emotional capacity to know any better."

After a year of dating, in August of 2003, Sullivan drove out to Nashua to spend a week with Nicole. By this time, they are both fed up with Nicole's mother's objections to their ideas of cohabitation.

"Our relationship was definitely emotionally abusive," Nicole said. "And I think now over time, from looking at it, my perspectives on that have changed so much. I feel like he is responsible for his actions and I am responsible for mine. I didn't really get that and I feel like in order to be emotionally abused, in order to stand for it and stay in it, there's gotta be something missing in you. There's gotta be something hurting already, something is not there, something's not right. And that needs to be figured out, found and fixed. Regardless of how a child is acting or what's coming off,there's more inside that kids need help with or guidance or just to have some type of connection with someone. You need to have relationships with people ahead of time, so that when the bad stuff does happen does happen you don't just come in to it expecting to work it out. Like, you need to have firm foundation with that person in order to work it out."

Nicole continued to side with Sullivan against her mother. The two argued constantly, Sullivan's influence quickly become apparent in Nicole's attitude toward her mother as she found fault with everything she did.

The two teens began discussing an unheard of option.

They began discussing the prospect of killing her mother.

"Well, this is where it starts getting...it's a scary business for me," Nicole said in a jailhouse interview. "I'll tell you that. I feel like I"m gonna cry. I don't talk about this stuff so this is really the first time. I think that my relationship with my mom was good. It was fine. I loved my mom. And...that changed. When...I'm not saying I stopped loving my mom, but...our relationship changed. I'm not gonna say that we were the most open because we weren't. We didn't talk about every little thing. I don't remember ever once talking about my parents' divorce with either of them. But the thing is, we didn't really talk about much of anything. When I was fourteen, I became involved with seventeen year old boy. This is really stemming into why I'm here (in jail) now."

OUT OF CONTROL

"Emotions begin to run high as Sullivan ups the ante in his hatred for Nicole's mother," Russo said. "Nicole is emotionally underdeveloped and has to choose between her mother and her 'man.' It is easy to look at it hindsight but with the teenaged girl's warp logic, she sees Sullivan as her entire world now. So she will do anything for him. Even murder."

Nicole's mom really didn't realize the danger that Sullivan was. She began doing what every mom does, demanding that her daughter stop seeing him, stop chatting with him and concentrate on her schoolwork. Nicole, on the other hand, remained fervent in her desire to move to Connecticut to move in with Sullivan.

"Jeanie, rightfully so, said 'you're fifteen you're finishing school,'" Wilson said. "'You're not moving to Connecticut' and that really upset both Nicole and Billy."

The prospect of not seeing Nicole had an adverse emotional effect on Billy.

"He started talking about killing himself...on the road...driving into a big truck because of leaving me..because of his sadness over it," Nicole recalled. "And I think now it just sounds silly, you know? But it wasn't then, and it was terrifying to me because I didn't...I didn't know how to...because of the way that our relationship was. Because he had become so much a part of my life. I mean, I really didn't feel like I was anything without him. I had nothing in my life at that time...I felt...at that time. So the thought of losing him in that way just wasn't okay with me. And that is unfortunately when conversations started about ultimately what happened. I guess I really I don't really go into too many details but I was sixteen and he was eighteen at that time. And I guess I should give you some background. He killed my mom and I was a part of it. I was not physically there but I knew and I helped him. I was, you know, going through the motions of what was being done. But mentally and emotionally, I don't think I was fully there. I don't think I was fully getting it."

"It was emotional manipulation," Russo said. "It is all so scary romantic for a fifteen year old girl to have some guy who is so in love with her that he is going to kill himself because he can't be with her. She has no one in her life to say 'this guy is a loser nutcase.' There isn't anyone that can talk sense to her. So she falls for the emotional manipulation of a highly disturbed but cunning con man."

Billy had convinced the depressed Nicole that her mother was an obstacle to both hers and his happiness.

"I really just did whatever I could to maintain that relationship because I didn't want to lose that," Nicole said. "I didn't want to lose him. And I quickly learned how it would go if I didn't always do everything that he wanted me to do. At that point...you know, getting to be fifteen...sixteen years old...I would fight more with my mom and there was a lot more to fight about, especially with, you know, this relationship that I was having with this kid."

THE FINAL PLAN

The couple tried different methods to murder Jeanne Domenico.

First they tried to poison Jeanne's coffee. The teens had placed Dimetapp, Benadryl and other drugs into Jeanne's coffee creamer in the refrigerator.

Jeanne used the creamer but didn't die and evidently remained ignorant of the plot on her life. The teens then added bleach to the creamer, wanting to strengthen the amount of poison. It was unclear in a court affidavit if Jeanne ever drank from the spiked creamer again.

The next idea was to set Nicole's mattress on fire with a candle. That idea didn't work because the bedding was made of fire retardant material.

It is unclear how the teens planned to fire up the mattress, whether they sneaked into her Nicole's bedroom and tried to fire up the mattress while she slept.

The third idea was to blow up the fuel oil tank in Jeanne's house. The teens had tied two ropes together which would serve as a wick. Their idea was to set fire to the rope which would then ignite a fire from the fuel tank. This idea was of course unsuccessful.

"These were hair-brained schemes from the start," Russo said, "particularly the fuel tank episode. What is interesting is that these are passive attacks. There is no face to face encounter with the mother, they just really want her gone. But it does show how these were test-runs of sorts. Sullivan was working up his nerve to do something violent. Nicole was building up her psyche. With each unsuccessful dry run, their determination and focus to do the job became greater until finally they realized that physical violence would be the only alternative."

THE ATTACK

The couple decided that Sullivan would do the killing. Nicole waited in the car at a local 7-Eleven where he mother worked part time to make ends meet. She wanted to wait there because she hated her home so much. Her boyfriend obliged, and entered the home of Jeanne Domenico between the hours of six and seven in the evening, waiting for her to come home from work.

The plan was for Billy to kill Jeanne by hitting her on the back of her head with a baseball bat.

Nicole waited anxiously in the car for an extended period of time then began to get worried as to why Sullivan was taking so long.

"Nicole called him and asked him what was taking so long," Wilson said. "Jeanne began getting upset that Nicole wasn't home and kept saying 'where is she? Tell her to come home.'"

Nicole heard her mother's voice on the other end of her cell phone telling her to "come home."

As became her habit, she did not listen to her mother.

"Sullivan did not attack Jeanne immediately," Russo said. "Again, he needed that fuel to add to his fire. So he confronted Jeanne, asking her why they kept refusing them to be together. Jeanne would speak logically like any adult would. She's underage. She's still in school. Of course, none of this would get into the head of Sullivan."

Jeanne made the mistake of turning her back on the young man. He then hit her across the back with the baseball bat.

"It looks as if Jeanne tried to get out of the kitchen door," Wilson said. "Billy started grabbing kitchen knives and attacking Jeanne with the steak knives from the state clock in the kitchen."

The attack was, in a word, brutal.

Sullivan stabbed Jeanne numerous times near her heart and stomach. He stabbed with such ferocity that the blade broke off the knife and he had to retrieve another. Then he stabbed her eight times in the throat.

"A number of the steak knives snapped off during the course of the attack," Wilson said.

According to later testimony by Sullivan, Jeanne managed to get a hold of one of the knives and tried to fight back. At this point, however, she is stunned and bleeding. Sullivan realizes that he is in trouble and goes in to finish the job.

Sullivan stabs her repeatedly as Jeanne tries to get away. A blade enters her lung.

"I'm done," were Jeanne's final words.

He then changed his clothes and cleaned the blood off. He then went back to Nicole, telling her to go inside the house to check for any weapons that he may have left behind. He also told her to get a towel.

The murder complete, Sullivan returned to the vehicle and announced that he had done the deal.

The couple, however, had a deal. It was now time for Nicole to do her part. She would help clean up the evidence left behind.

"The fact that she could go and clean up after Billy had killed her mother," Wilson said. "She had to have hit her mother with the door. And then she had to have stepped over her body to clean up for her boyfriend. That she was able to do that was chilling to do me."

Nicole took a cloth and began clean up her mother's blood from the kitchen floor.

"The fact that a psychopath like Sullivan was able to stab Jeanne to death isn't the most blood curdling aspect of this case," Russo said. "The really scary part is how Nicole was able to go back into that house, see her mother laying in a pool of blood on the kitchen floor, then begin to do her end of the bargain, which was to clean up after her boyfriend. The amount of psychological and emotional disconnect here is chilling."

The two then hid the evidence in the outskirts around town before going to a shopping mall in order for Sullivan to purchase new clothes.

Hours after the killing, Nicole finally began to realize the gravity of what has taken place. She realizes that she and Billy were not going off to "see the world." Her best friend, her mother was gone forever.

Jeanne's body would be discovered by her boyfriend later that evening and he quickly called the police. At around 10:15 p.m., Sergeant William Moore and Detective Shawn Hill saw Sullivan and Nicole approach the crime scene.

"They were cocky enough to think they could outwit the cops," Russo said. "By approaching the crime scene and acting all innocent, not knowing what happened, they thought they would deflect attention away from themselves. It really shows you how dumb these two kids were."

The police then stated the teens would have to be separated for an interview. Nicole protested, stating that Sullivan would not know how to get to the police station. The police informed her that they would take him there themselves.

"This is when things start to go haywire in their heads," Russo said. "Nicole is getting nervous, knowing that they will be questioned separately and face the prospect of not having their stories straight. These two were not exactly forward thinking individuals."

The two waited for the police cruisers to arrive and made conversation with Detective Moore. The detective noted that Sullivan did most all of the talking and admitted that he did not like police officers, stating that he had been charged before with crimes he did not commit.

Moore informed Sullivan that he would be given a "fair shake" in the questioning.

Sullivan, however, kept talking. He informed the detective that he had been shopping for souvenirs with Nicole that day and talked about Jeanne's relationship with Nicole. The detective said that Sullivan paced back and forth and then sat down on the trunk of his car.

Twelve minutes later, Detective Linehan arrived on the scene, making contact with both Nicole and Sullivan. Linehan noticed how nervous and "jumpy" Sullivan was. Linehan told Sullivan to "relax" and then the teen explained that he suffered from anxiety but did not need medication. He told the police that he had "no problem" to come to the station for questioning.

Linehan sat with Sullivan in the back seat of the squad car as they headed back to the station. Both of the teens were having casual conversations with the officers but after being questioned separately, they both admitted their involvement, leading police to the locations where they had disposed of the evidence.

"Both of the teenage lovers wilted under the police interrogations," Russo said. "She immediately ratted out Sullivan as the killer while he did the same to her. There was no loyalty for one another while under the police questioning."

Sullivan would be convicted of first degree murder, sentenced to life without parole.

Sullivan, however, did not let his Lothario ways go to rust in jail. He wrote love letters to a girl named Monique Teal who was then sixteen. This occurred while Sullivan was awaiting trial and later Teal's testimony was used in court.

Teal, using a pen name of Monique Sullivan in her love letters to Sullivan, had agreed to a date to marry the now twenty-year old murderer. Teal's mother, however, found out about the letters and forbade him to call or write.

"He just laughed about it," she said. "He said that no matter what my mom would say or do that nothing could keep us away from each other."

"You see him trying the same techniques on Teal," Russo said. "The immediate declarations of love. The flowery language. The idea of them against the world. In Teal's case, however, her mother put a stop to it."

Sullivan admitted to the Jeanne Domenico killing in one of his letters to her, Teal would reveal, although she didn't read from the letter in court. She said she obeyed Sullivan's demands and threw that letter away.

JAIL LIFE

Nicole Kasinskas would plead guilty to second-degree murder.

"My original sentence was forty years to life," Nicole said. "It is now thirty-seven years and a half to life based on a plea that if I acquired my GED I would get two and a half years off. I don't mark days off on my calendar. I don't do those types of things. This is my life now and I want to live it. I don't want to just look at it as one day down closer to my real life. Like this is my real life. I smile a lot and I live a lot and I'm happy a lot and I just prefer it that way rather than get lost in the sadness of it because you can. And I have. But if I...if I can choose not to...if I can be stronger than than then I want to. And it makes me feel freer. It makes me feel that I have more control of my life."

"Her life as a promising honor roll student at fifteen years old with her mother who loved her very much," Wilson said. "She lost her entire life. And for what?"

"I had no goals. I had no hopes and dreams, you know? You need to have your own hobbies and friends and stuff. Outside the relationship, there needs to be that balance. I just never had that, I never figured that out."

"Maybe if someone had said something like, 'I see you, I see that there's more to you than this and I want to see more of you. I'm here for you. I care about you.' I mean everyone needs help, everyone needs support."

KILLER NURSE :

THE TRUE STORY OF GENENE JONES

78

KORI MAYER

Genene Anne Jones was born on July 13th, 1950 in Texas but was given up for adoption. Her adopted parents had three other children. Two were older and one was younger than Genene.

EARLY LIFE

Her adopted parents were Richard and Gladys Jones. Richard, better known as "Dick", a night club and was a gambler. He was a big spender and generous when he was flush. His club was called the Kit Kat Swim Club, the place had a dance floor with a patio and pool outside. His wife Gladys was the disc jockey at the club and the couple lived an extravagant lifestyle. They had a mansion that looked down on San Antonio, would travel often and they would both have pilot licenses .

At the age of ten, however, Genene's father was arrested for stealing the safe of a customer who had been at Jones' club at the time of the robbery. These charges were later dropped.

It could have been due to intimidation on Dick's part. The man was six feet tall, weighed a solid 240 pounds and was bold. He had an aggressive demeanor when needed and his adopted daughter developed the same traits.

His business soon failed, however. The shady Kit Kat Club soon turned into a family themed restaurant which put Dick further into debt. He then sold off the restaurant and earned a living putting up billboards around San Antonio. Genene would later describe helping her father put up the billboards as one of the happier times of her life.

Still, Genene felt as if she suffered from neglect in the adopted home. The parents had paired off the four kids on the basis of age. Genene had an older brother Wiley and an older sister named Lisa. She had a younger brother named Travis who had a learning disability that she doted on and cared for. Nonetheless, she felt jealous of all the attention that Lisa would receive. Genene referred to herself as the "black sheep" of the family and took out her frustrations on her classmates at school. She worked in the library at John Marshall and was described as "kind of bossy" by the high school librarian as she would berate other student volunteers who weren't doing their jobs up to her standards. Short and chubby, Genene felt unattractive and began to become known for lying and manipulating people.

"Lying was like talking for her," one of her classmates recalled as Genene would often tell people that she was related to Micky Dolenz, the band member of the Monkees, and that she would routinely have phone conversations with him all the time.

Tragedy would strike in her teens, however, when her younger brother Travis died in a freak accident.

He had put together a pipe bomb which exploded in his face, sending metal shards into his head. Genene took the loss hard, arriving at the funeral with a large flower wreath, crying hysterically, then feinting.

"You wonder when Genene's mind got twisted," forensic psychologist Dina Foster said. "It had to have been early on in her development when somehow, someway she got a surge of power when she was care taking for someone particularly a child. This was probably her brother, Travis. Being a caregiver for him made her feel important. She realized that she could be respected and have people look up to her until it became twisted."

A year later, her father died of cancer at the age of 56 which further devastated Genene. She had yet to graduate high school and wanted to get married. Her adopted mother refused as she Genene's choice of mate, a dropout named James "Jimmy" Harvey Delany Jr as nothing but trouble.

The two would marry, however, and live in a guesthouse near the mansion. Jimmy, however, was only interested in cars and drinking. The two would squabble often until Jimmy decided to join the Navy. With her husband away a basic training, Genene would not remain faithful, going after both single and married men. She had an affair with the newlywed husband of a former high school classmate. Then she began to tell people she had been sexually abused as a child. After four years of marriage, Genene divorced Jimmy as she stated that he had been physically abusive toward her.

Genene would threaten divorce but the two would reconcile.

"She experienced abandonment twice," Foster said. "The first go around was when her mother gave her up for adoption. The second go around was when her brothers and father died back to back. She had lost two loved ones to illnesses and one to a tragic accident. She felt helpless and out of control. But unlike most people, Genene went the criminal route in order to assuage the pain. She had to do things to get the power and control back."

CAREER LIFE & DIVORCE

Genene entered Mim's Beauty School and became a beautician, finding work at the Methodist Hospital beauty parlor. She had her first child, Richard, in 1972 while she and Jimmy were stationed in Georgia. They would move back to San Antonio but by that time the marriage was failing. She filed for divorce in Bexar County, eight months after Richard was born and stated that her husband was "a man of violent and ungovernable temper and passion" while also accusing him of "unconscionable brutality and physical cruelty." She won a court order that forbade her husband from going near both her or baby Richard. Two months later, however, the couple had gotten back together and the judge threw out the divorce suit.

"Clearly they had an on and off again relationship," Foster said. "Jimmy was hapless, wanting to do nothing more than race cars and party. So in some aspects Genene had found her soul mate, a man who needed taking care of."

But on June 3rd, 1974, Genene filed for divorce again and the couple would battle in the court system for three more years. She would file suit against Delany for failure to pay child support and in August of 1976 she won a contempt citation against him. In March of 1977, both consented to drop the legal battle and in July 17 of 1977 Genene's second child, Heather, was born. She later admitted that Heather had been conceived out of wedlock when she and Delany had another brief coming to terms.

Genene would then move back in with her adopted mother who helped with the babies as she began her training at San Antonio Independent School District's School of Vocational Nursing. Genene was a mediocre high school student but she excelled in the program, earning high grades. She aced the licensing exam and got a job at Methodist Hospital.

Genene only lasted eight months, however, getting fired when she made decisions about patient care in which she had no authority as well as being rude to patients. Genene would later claim that she was fired for standing up to a doctor who was being rude to a patient.

"She was a compulsive liar when she was a kid," Foster said. "And the lying continued into her adult life as it turned into full blown denial. She was never at fault for anything. It was always someone else, doctors, nurses, her mother, her husband. She never lived in the land of responsibility."

REIGN OF TERROR BEGINS

Genene then found work at Bexar County Hospital (now known as the University Hospital of San Antonio) where she was assigned to the Pediatric ICU.

It is here where the trouble officially began.

Her first patient had a fatal stomach disease called necrotizing enterocolitis and the boy died after surgery. Genene did not handle it well, crying hysterically. "She just went berserk," Cherylyn Pendergraft said, the RN that was orienting Genene during this time. Genene went so far as to move a stool toward the baby's cubicle and just sat there staring at the body.

Pendergraft felt the gesture odd considering that Genene had barely cared for the child.

Nonetheless, Genene saw herself as an equal to the RN's on duty and worked extra hard to acquire more knowledge than an ordinary LVN.

She worked the graveyard shift upon hire then transferred to the swing shift where she worked f3 p.m to 11 p.m while frequently volunteering for overtime and extra shifts.

Genene soon took on a reputation as the "nurse who cried wolf" to the many resident doctors who were training at the hospital. She would issue warnings about a child's worsening condition to the intern. If the intern did nothing she would then go to the resident doctor. If that physician did nothing then she would go higher up the chain of command and wouldn't stop until her recommendations were addressed.

Despite her eagerness to be perceived as on the same level as a registered nurse, Genene would skip continuation classes on the proper use of pharmaceuticals. In her first year, she was written up on eight separate occasions for giving the wrong dosage.

Genene wouldn't let any reprimands stop her, however, as she soon became the ward bully in the cramped quarters of the pediatric ICU. She would intimidate other nurses with her coarse demeanor, making more than a few transfer out of the unit to get away from her.

Her bullying tactics enabled her to make the unit her own, as she was the foul-mouthed Queen of the ward, bragging about her sexual escapades and making inappropriate remarks.

"Here we see the beginnings of tacit approval," Foster said. "No one at the hospital wants to put themselves on the line to stand up against her. It is an environment where everyone is trying to cover their own ass. No one wants to play snitch even when this woman is saying and doing all of these inappropriate things."

Even more disturbing is that Genene would also predict which baby would die.

During "report", a time in which the nurses would describe the conditions of their patients during the shift change handover to the next nurse, Genene would play the role of the Grim Reaper.

"This patient is really bad," she'd say forewarning the nurse, or even predicting death."This patient isn't going to make it."

By 1981, Genene would always demand to be assigned to the sickest patients. She seemed to enjoy the adrenaline rush of the code blues and would grieve when the child expired. Genene would hold the dead bodies and sing to it, making sure she would be the one to take the corpse to the morgue.

"She had a twisted hero complex," Foster said. "She thought of herself as equal to any RN. Most LVNs defer to the registered nurses out of education and experience. But it was quite the opposite with Genene. When the shit hit the fan she would be the first to come to the rescue. The problem was that she created these situations where she could be seen as the hero. Remember she didn't give them enough medication to kill them outright. She gave the babies just enough of a dose so that they would go into cardiac arrest. She wanted to be seen as the savior to the parents of the children she was killing. She wanted to be seen as the hero of the ward. This need was so deep-seated that she was willing to kill to get that need met. That need to be seen as a hero. That need to be seen as the most compassionate of all."

TOO MANY PATIENTS DYING

Co-workers became concerned that a surprising number of patients under the care of Jones were dying.

"The other nurses became concerned," said Vincent J.M. Dimaio, the chief medical examiner at the time. "That there were increased numbers of cardiopulmonary arrests on the ward. All her victims were children. The most innocent of the population. This would not have happened if the cases had been reported to the medical examiner's office."

Unlike most hospitals, Bexar County didn't lock their medications in a cabinet. When it become apparent that children were dying in the unit from non-fatal illnesses, the hospital dragged its feet in an investigation. There was a two-week period where seven children died in the unit. These deaths occurred only when Genene Jones was on duty and the patients were under her care.

"Astonishing," Foster said. "The tacit approval now extended to the cover up of children being murdered. The hospital administrators put their own public relations and jobs above the lives of children. It is a travesty of justice that no one at the hospital was ever punished for this."

Genene had an ally in the department in the form of Dr. James Robotham, however. Known as "JR", a reference to the ruthless businessman from the TV show Dallas, Robotham was an aggressive doctor throughout his tenure in the ICU. He had no problem dressing down nurses or student doctors who were not up to snuff or did not bend to his will. He had no hiring authority in the hospital but took on a vital role throughout the ICU by placing the patient's care onto his shoulders.

Genene saw a kindred spirit in Robotham and the doctor took a liking to her. There was one occasion in which he needed assistance and chose Genene over another nurse.

"She had been validated," Foster said. "She also wanted to be acknowledged for her nursing talents and finally there was someone who came along and anointed her as someone who was worthy."

"Robotham's Pet" as some of the nurses would later call her, would nonetheless display a macabre interest when a child came in with a fatal illness. Genene would make it clear that she wanted to be on hand when death inevitably came.

Genene would enjoy calling the parents to inform them of their child's death, sharing in their grief over the phone.

"She was Jekyll and Hyde," Foster said. "With the nurses and staff she would be coarse, demanding and condescending. But with the parents of the children she turned into the ultimate caregiver. Soft-spoken, compassionate, and joining them in their pain. She would have the parents believing that she was the most caring person on the face of the earth."

Never mind the fact that she would orchestrate the medical emergency of the child.

"That was her way of getting attention," Dimaio said. "She was a 'big person'. She was a 'big person' when she resuscitated children. When she brought them back from death's door. And the rest of her life, she wasn't anything."

THE KILLINGS MOUNT

A six month old baby named Jose Antonio Flores came into the unit with non-fatal symptoms: fever, vomiting and diarrhea. Unfortunately, he came under the care of Genene.

The baby soon suffered a seizure went into cardiac arrest and died.

Genene grabbed the dead baby and ran out of the department with the staff having to track down the crying LVN. The infant was later blood-tested and the results revealed that there had been an overdose of heparin, an anti-coagulant.

No one had ordered that the drug be administered and now the staff became suspicious.

When questioned about the baby's death, Genene resorted to manipulation and blackmail. She told the staff that she took records on every child that had died there and she knew which doctor had killed them.

Finally, one of the doctors informed the hospital administration what he suspected of Genene Jones. He had found a book in her possession about how to inject heparin through the skin without leaving a mark.

The hospital administrators, however, did not want the bad public relations fall out that would result from being a hospital that had a reputation for infant deaths.

"Say that they expected one (death) a week," Dimaio said. "All of a sudden they were getting three or four or five a week. I don't think there was any doubt that they had a good idea of what she (Genene) was doing."

"The amazing thing here is that even after the incident with the Flores' baby, Genene was allowed to continue working on the ward," Foster said.

Another child came into Genene's unit, this time to recover from open heart surgery. The child made progress but during Genene's shift he died.

"They notice that all of them (the deaths) were on the same shift," Dimaio said. "And all of them involved patients being taken care of by Genene Jones."

More doctors complained and a committee was set up to investigate. Head nurse Pat Belko and James Robotham were in charge on the hospital end but an outside team of investigators came in to look at the problem.

This third party team declined to put the blame on Genene as their findings were inconclusive.

COVERING THEIR ASS

Confident of they were in the clear, the hospital reports no abnormal deaths to the county medical examiner. Still, the hospital knew that Genene Jones was responsible for the deaths.

"She was left on the ward even though they knew what was going on," Dimaio said. "Someone said why don't we just fire her? Then they said well she'll just sue us and they'll be a big scandal. There were more interested in saving their reputation and not being sued then in the life and health of these children."

In order to avoid a public relations debacle, the administration decided to replace the LVNs in the unit with registered nurses. They said they were raising the "training bar" for ICU nurses and that LVNs would no longer be needed.

"So when they adopted that policy they let her go from that unit," Dimaio said. "Let go by the way, with an excellent letter of recommendation. Even though they knew what was going on."

Genene had been suspected in the deaths of over 47 other children, the NYT noted that the administration of Bexar County Medical Center and the University of Texas Medical school had shredded over 9,000 pounds of pharmaceutical records, records that were created during the time when Jones worked there.

By doing this, these administrators effectively destroyed any evidence that would be helpful in convicting Genene Jones of more crimes. The hospital stated that the shredding of documents was "routine" and a "coincidence", but the district attorney was able to intervene when, acting on a tip from an informant, he stopped the hospital from destroying an additional 50,000 pounds of pharmaceutical and medical records. The dean of medicine at Bexar was then cited for contempt of court when it was discovered that she withheld hospital reports from the grand jury.

"This is certainly an indictment of the hospital," Foster said. "If over 47 children were murdered, than there would have to be justice. The irony here is that the hospital administrators are not that far off from Genene Jones' mindset. They lie, deny and keep things in secret. All for the sake of control. All for the sake of being perceived that they are something they are not. Genene wanted to be seen as a hero but was really a killer. The hospital wants good pr at all costs, even childcare's lives. They are scum."

THE MURDERS CONTINUE

After her release from the county hospital and with a letter of recommendation in hand, Jones found work at a pediatric physician's clinic in Kerrville, Texas.

"She ended up here in Kerrville after she left San Antonio because of all these unexplained deaths," district attorney Ron Sutton said. "Genene Jones absolutely despises me because I brought down her little self-constructed impact."

The clinic was a start-up to be run by Dr. Kathleen Holland. She only had budget for an LVN and immediately thought of Genene Jones. She had remembered Genene and had been impressed by her take-charge personality and competence.

Holland contacted the human resource office at the hospital and inquired about the availability of Genene. Holland knew about the strange rumors about Genene but was willing to overlook them as she needed someone who could bring passion to their start up.

Holland didn't know how true those weird rumors were..

"She would create these medical emergencies," District Attorney Ron Sutton said. "That only she would know to handle. Then she would look like this supreme nurse when she would take care of the emergencies that she created."

Holland's revelation began with Petti McClellan brought in her young daughter Chelsea. McClellan said that Chelsea had a "bad cold" and went into the exam room with Dr. Holland. Genene then took the young baby out of Chelsea's arms, stating that she was going to "play" with the baby so that she and the doctor could talk.

"She had an irresistible compulsion," Foster said. "Doesn't matter where she is at, a hospital, a clinic, she has that compulsion. She'll see the opportunity to be a create the scenario for herself and she takes it."

"The protocol for the doctor's office would be the nurse, Genene Jones, would take the baby into a separate room just she and the baby, to perform whatever cursory examination; weight, blood pressure, whatever," Sutton said. "But during the time Genene would have these children by themselves all of a sudden they would become like a rag doll. And then she would scream out 'the baby's not breathing.'"

Moments later, Genene would cry out for help, saying that the baby couldn't breathe.

Doctor Holland immediately jumped into action, seeing that the baby had gone into a seizure. The child would be transported to a hospital and her life was spared.

The McClellan's expressed their gratitude toward Holland and Genene. They thought the world of the duo, believing that they saved the life of their child.

Little did they know that Genene had injected the child with succinylcholine.

Genene had used various methods to kill children under her care. She used injections of digoxin, heparin and later succinylcholine to cause a "code blue" in her patients. She would revive them afterward and receive praise. The succinylcholine she used is a paralytic that causes a temporary paralysis of skeleton muscles which can affect a patient's breathing. When she injected small children with this drug, the victim would suffer from cardiac arrest.

Petti would later return to the clinic months later with Chelsea. She had actually called the clinic to make an appointment for her son Cameron but Holland insisted that she bring Chelsea in so that she could "check on her."

"My daughter wasn't sick," Petti would later say.

Holland later disputes the claim that she asked Petti to bring Chelsea in instead of Cameron.

Unfortunately, Petti would bring Chelsea in and witness Genene administer two shots. The second shot would cause Chelsea to go into a seizure and later die.

"Once she began doing it," Foster said. "She couldn't stop. She became fueled by the adrenaline. The rush she got by sticking the syringe into the baby. The rush she got in waiting for the child to go into cardiac arrest. The the rush she got by watching the child die and comforting it in its death. She even got off on informing the parents of the baby's death. That is how twisted her mind was."

"Her original intent may not have been to kill," Foster said. "She was all about being seen as the hero, the Superwoman who came into save the day. Why she would target the same child coming in for another routine check-up really shows that she was getting careless about her victims. She had gotten away with it for so long that she didn't care. Plus, the compulsion would override whatever logic and forward thinking she had."

Chelsea's death was initially seen as sudden infant death syndrome.

"That's when we talked to the anesthesiologist," Sutton said. "He said that this child looks like it was coming out from the effects of succinylcholine, and we launched our investigation at that point."

"Soon as she got that first shot," Petti McClellan said, "Chelsey immediately starting reacting to it. And I asked her right off the bat, 'what did you do? What did you do? Something's wrong with her.'."

Genene visited Chelsey's grave and seemed genuinely remorseful.

"She was a psychopath with conflicted emotions," Foster said. "On one hand she had this need to kill and be in control of what others thought of her, specifically as a hero. And the other hand, she may have felt remorse when her 'heroic' efforts didn't produce the results she wanted."

Chelsey's mother, Petti, however, was shocked to see Genene at her daughter's grave.

Holland would later find puncture marks in a bottle of succinylcholine in a storage cabinet that only she and Genene had access to. "There were two holes in the lid of this bottle," Sutton said. "One where she had withdrawn and then she attempted to replace it with saline solution."

With the investigators closing in, Genene began to panic. She arrived at the clinic after lunch and complained to Holland that she was feeling ill...She had overdosed on her anti-depressants and began looking lethargic.

Holland immediately called the paramedics and Genene's stomach was pumped. Later upon her release, Texas Ranger Joe Davis interrogated her about the holes in the bottle of succinylcholine. Genene denied involvement, stating that she would be willing take a polygraph test.

The next day, Holland was shocked to see Genene report for work as if nothing had happened. She then informed Genene that her services would no longer be needed. Genene grew enraged and challenged Holland to take a polygraph. She then stormed out of the office.

Genene would later call back to the office and informed Holland's secretary that she had left a letter for the physician in her drawer.

The letter was a one page suicide note that she had written before she had taken the overdose of anti-depressants.

"There isn't anyway to explain to you why things are going to change. Sometimes, as wrong as it may seem, you have to except what life dishes out.

When your older, and I know your tired of hearing that, but you will be able to understand why, why I have to go away. It doesn't mean I don't love you. Please believe that. No amount of money or worldly goods could every buy my love. It is so deep & strong, it will last for all eternity.

Please explain if you can to Heather & Michael how much I love them. It's such a strong love, I can't put it on paper. I know I'm asking a lot, but I really feel your the only one who could do it.

I'm not guilty of murder, & I hope you believe that. But Daddy's way is right. It takes all the pressure off you and the seven people whose life I have altered.

No one can hurt me with my Daddy. He'll straighten this whole thing out & then we'll go home & everything will be alright. No more problems for you, no more nightmares for me.

Please make sure Michael and Heather are not separated. I know how my mother feels about Heather, but I also know how she feels about Michael. If Debbie or you can't take them together, please be sure whoever does are good people. People with lots of love.

Please don't be angry. I'm going with Daddy because I miss him and I want to be with him. He'll take care of both of us.

You'll be fine. Please believe that.

I love you,

Genene

Genene had attempted to frame Holland for the murders but all evidence pointed to her. All said and done, Genene had poisoned at least six children at the clinic. Three of the parents continued to utilize Holland as their pediatrician while three other families sued both Holland and Genene Jones as they believed that Holland knew or should have known about Genene's murderous ways.

The criminal investigation began and Chelsea's body was exhumed, revealing traces of the succinylcholine.

Her exact numbers of victims remain unknown as hospital officials first "misplaced" then destroyed records of her activities to prevent lawsuits after Genene's first conviction.

Genene would go on trial on January 15th, 1984 for the murder of Chelsea and injury to the other children. On February, 15, 1984, Genene was convicted of murder after a three hour deliberation. She was given the maximum sentence of ninety-nine years. In October, she went on trail for injuring Rolando Jones with an injection of heparin. She was sentenced a total of 159 years with the possibility of parole that came up after serving ten years.

In 1985, Gene was sentenced to 99 years in prison for killing fifteen month old Chelsea McClellan.

Later that year, she was sentenced to a term of sixty years in prison for the attempted murder of Rolando Jones with heparin.

"I've had several cases that stand out in my mind," Sutton said. "But this one is particularly heinous because of death to small children."

SERIAL KILLER TO BE RELEASED

Genene Jones is now set to go free because of a legal loophole in the form of She is now scheduled for mandatory release in February 2018 due to a Texas law that prevents prison overcrowding. Genene has been a prisoner who has exhibited "good behavior", becoming eligible for the release.

"Please, please, please, do not let this person walk," Petti McClellan said.

"Genene Jones is probably one of the worst types of serial killers because keep in mind who her victims were," said Andy Kahan, a victim advocate. "Defenseless, voiceless, babies. One of the nation's most diabolical serial killers in our country's history is set to be legally released,"

"I was so angry that it went on for so long," Cherlyn Pendergraft said. "That so many children had to die."

Jones now claims to be sickly and is housed in medical jail unit.

"Am I prepared that she walks?" McClellan asked. "No. Because she's gonna hurt another child. I don't want to hear that she's sick. Or that she's old, she's two years older than I am."

"There is absolutely no reason for Genene Jones to be walking the streets," Foster said. "She has a compulsion that has to be satiated. She needs to be locked up for the rest of her life."

The current District Attorney is looking to re-open old cases against Jones in order to keep her in prison.

LESBIAN VAMPIRE KILLER :

THE TRUE STORY OF TRACEY WIGGINTON

TRISH SAMUELSON

The mutilated body of 47-year old Brisbane council worker Edward Baldock was found on the morning of October 22nd, 1989 in Kangaroo Park. He was naked, stabbed multiple times and had his throat slashed so severely he was nearly decapitated.

The perpetrator was a woman named Tracey Wigginton, a violent lesbian who reportedly drank her victim's blood after she had severed his throat.

The killing was dubbed the Lesbian Vampire Murder and it sent shock waves through the entire country of Australia.

EARLY LIFE

Tracey Wigginton was born in 1965 and raised in a small northern coastal city called Rockhampton. Her mother had been adopted early on, raised by an affluent couple by the names of George and Avril Wigginton. The Wiggintons had two other adopted daughters, Dorrell and later Michelle.

Avril would brutalize the young girls, abusing them without mercy. She would often whip them with electrical cords and a chained hose.

She also hated men.

"When you grow up, men will do horrible things to you," Avril would warn her young adopted daughters. "All they want is sex."

She would save all of her affection and love for her pet chihuahua which she carried around like a baby.

The girls would remain indoors for the most part while under the care of the Wiggintons. Rhonda, however, would leave home in 1965 to marry Bill Rossborough and give birth to her daughter Tracey.

The man would prove to be a drifter and leave Rhonda less than a year after they were married. Rhonda would be forced back to live in the home of her adopted parents.

She then met a man from out of town and decided to live with him. Rhonda left Tracey in the care of her own adopted parents while she was only four years old and three years later the Wiggintons formally adopted the young Tracey.

GOLDEN CHILD OR BLACK SHEEP?

Unlike her mother and the other adopted siblings in the home, Tracey would be spoiled by her grandparents. She had another sister during this time, a girl named Michelle who was older and half-Indian.

While the grandparents doted on Tracey, Michelle would be the subject of routine beatings. Avril would whip her and once locked her in a dog kennel overnight.

This abuse troubled Tracey greatly as she had formed a bond with her adopted sister. Avril would do everything to keep the two from becoming close, often telling Tracey that Michelle was a "bad influence" and that Tracey was not allowed to play with her.

Later, Michelle was blamed for something Tracey did and ran away from the Wigginton home at the age of sixteen.

Tracey has stated publicly that she "loved her grandfather dearly" but also claimed that he started to demand sex with her after she turned eight (she had informed a fellow classmate about the abuse at the age of ten.)

SCHOOL TROUBLE

The Wiggintons paid for Tracey to have private schooling. She learned art, music and dance. Her troubles started to mount in junior high, however, when she was expelled for allegedly "molesting other girls."

"Her childhood was in a word, horrid," forensic psychologist Gary Harding said. "There were unsubstantiated rumor that her father abused her. What is certain is that Tracey had been abandoned by her mother and was subject to the constant misandry of her adopted grandmother. Avril hated men and certainly passed that down to Wigginton. The incidents of molesting other students could be an indication of her repeating her own abuse, certainly. Because of her size, she would always have been one of the biggest students in the class and certainly the biggest girl. She may have been acting out to gain power and experimenting with her sexuality."

Students were afraid of her as one student commented "I'd always stay clear of her – she had that strange evil look."

Tracey was then sent to a Catholic convent school (Range Catholic School) but wound up dropping out of the institution.

She had grown to be a large young woman, 5'10" and weighing over 240 lbs. During her trial, one news reporter described her as having a "huge buttocks and thighs."

"The physical transformation was simply astonishing," Harding said. "It is no exaggeration to say that Tracey looked like a super sweet and cute kid. Long hair, earrings and long dresses. You compare and contrast her childhood photos to the woman she became and it brings a tear to your eye."

DEATH AND INHERITANCE

Wigginton's adopted parents would die within two years of one another, leaving her devastated.

Abandoned by those closest around her through death or choice, Wigginton would carry around a security blanket with her throughout the rest of her life. This would come in the form of an old pillowcase she called her "bi-lo." She would twirl the material around her hands and caress her face with it. When she didn't know the whereabouts of "bi-lo" she would become hysterical and search around frantically for her security blanket. Sometimes she would wear it under her clothes, around her neck like a scar and place it under her pillow when she slept.

"Of course the security blanket screams abandonment issues," Harding said. "She needs a constant in her life. Something she could count on to always be the 'same', so to speak. So that pillow case became her security but unlike most children who utilize such a psychological tool, she never grew out of it."

Tracey would receive a sizable inheritance, getting an initial payment of $75,000 which she blew through on clothes and a motorcycle. After the death of her parents, she went over to her aunt Dorrell's house and painted the walls with swastikas and obscenities.

PERSONALITY TRANSFORMATION

Wigginton's look would slowly change from a sweet-faced, long haired girl who had numerous boyfriends to an intimidating "butch" obsessed with the occult.

Her roommate was the first to notice the change in Wigginton. A gifted artist, Tracey would often draw roses and other flowers in bright, happy depictions. As time went on, however, her art became darker. She started creating "frightening, mythical monsters" while drawing pentagrams constantly with different demons and gargoyles around them. She would eventually carve a pentagram into the back of her hand with a knife.

Her physical transformation was gradual as she would cut her hair shorter and shorter until she had a full military buzz cut. She stopped wearing anything feminine like dresses and heels, instead electing to wearing masculine looking jeans and tops.

Wigginton adopted an all black look, with leather jacket and calf length boots.

In her left boot, she carried a knife.

"Physically the butch in Tracey was beginning to appear," Gagliardi wrote in Lust for Blood. "Short, spiky hair hair, predominantly black outfits, studded leather. On one occasion she returned to Range College in an army uniform offering 'to smarten the kids up.'"

Her interest in the occult became all too apparent as she would wear a circular silver belt buckle with a five-pointed star inside. The tattoos on her body included a black rose on her right upper arm, a large Merlin on her left upper arm, the Eye of Horus on her left hand and another knife-etched pentagram on her right hand.

She purchased a motorcycle from her inheritance and squandered the rest on booze and bar hopping. Wigginton soon became known in lesbian circles as "Bobby" or as some described her as the "big butch bitch from up on the hill."

"It isn't uncommon for people to rename themselves when they want an identity change," Harding said. "In Wigginton's case, however, it may have been a case of multiple personality disorder. Her 'Bobby' persona may have gotten so strong that it overtook other aspects of her personality. The 'Bobby' persona is what gave her power and strength while 'Little Tracey' was helpless, useless and abandoned."

LEAVING SCHOOL

Wigginton would drop out of school at the age of seventeen in 1982. She would have a dust-up with her biological mother, punching her in the face. She then met a bisexual woman in a bar named "Sunshine". Sunshine was the opposite of Wigginton, petite, blonde and with the ability to draw attention from men and lesbians alike. The two began dating but Sunshine would often cheat on Tracey with other men, leaving Wigginton hurt and humiliated. Despite the cheating, Wigginton would press Sunshine for marriage and the two would exchange vows in a ceremony conducted by a Hare Krishna.

Four years later, she would inherit another $75,000 from her adoptive parents estate.

Tracey burned through the cash quickly as she moved to a seaside resort town called Cairns. Needing money, she found work as a bouncer in a gay nightclub.

She briefly returned to school, starting a course in hospitality but it wasn't long before she dropped out. Her "marriage" to Sunshine fizzled as the blonde woman left her for another man. Devastated, she asked the owner of the club where she worked to impregnate her. They would have intercourse in front of a group of "six close friends" and Tracey would become pregnant but lose the baby in a miscarriage.

"There really isn't any surprise that Tracey would burn through the $75,000," Harding said. "What is surprising however is the fact that she would adopt such a submissive role to Sunshine. Playing the part of the dutiful man, it sounds like the woman's bisexuality didn't sit too well with Wigginton. She would spend long hours sleeping in a fetal position after the two would fight or she would find out that Sunshine was with a man."

ASSEMBLING THE TEAM

Wigginton remained fascinated by the black arts. She held seances, read tarot cards and was eventually able to surround herself with a group of lesbian friends who had similar interests.

"Tracey was one of those people who took diametrical opposition to her own upbringing," Australian forensic psychologist Gary Harding said. "She wanted to rebel against her family, her grandmother, mother and their Catholicism. She thought it better to embrace the exact opposite of the religion of the family of her choice, the dark arts if you will. It is a form of defiance, a form of control. The older she got the more she wanted control so the more she got involved in the occult. When she did this, she was able to attract a group of young women who felt the same way."

"Tracy Wigginton had a personality to match her 17 stone (240 lbs) frame – big," wrote Gagliardi in Lust for Blood. "She died her hair midnight blue and tattooed her body. She was deeply committed to all her causes: lesbianism, occultism and devil-worship. Before long she had coerced her friends from the Valley to kill for her."

Wigginton assembled a group of lesbian friends which included Lisa Ptaschinski, Kim Jervis, and Tracey Waugh. All three of the women fell for the charm of Wigginton who dazzled them with her stories and knowledge of the occult.

Part of the reason Wigginton was able to get these women under her spell was through intimidation. She had convinced her girlfriend Lisa that she had the "ability to disappear except for her eyes."

"Wigginton was a devil worshiper who could disappear," Waugh said, dovetailing Lisa's sentiment. "Leaving only her 'cat's eyes' visible."

The women all dressed alike, wearing black leather outfits and black t-shirts. They would meet in graveyards and drink, holding seances.

During one meeting, Wigginton instructed them that she needed "fresh blood" and that they need to find her a victim.

"Wigginton loved holding court," Harding said. "Not only was her physique much larger than the rest of the young women, her personality was as well. She liked going on rants about the devil and her own vampirism. The other girls were in awe of her."

"Tracey Wigginton was the main instigator," criminal attorney Adrian Gundelach said. "She was telling these girls and leading them on the path to believe that she was a vampire. And that she needed human blood to keep going."

"There was a lot of buzz in the media about all of the women being lesbians," Harding said. "Remember this murder took place in the late 1980s so there was still a lot of judgment and taboo surrounding this sexual preference. Lesbianism was thought of as an aberrant behavior and Wigginton looked to play the stereotypical role of the violent butch who sought to dominate their partners rather than give pleasure."

"Initially, the media reported that Baldock was the victim of a group of man-hating, devil worshiping lesbians. They described Wigginton as being this beast, which she was, but the fact that she was both a lesbian and a vampire gave the story a lurid feel, and the media took full advantage."

A FULL-FLEDGED VAMPIRE

During interviews with police, Kim Jervis would state that Wigginton had captured bats and kept the creatures in her house. Remaining true to all of the vampire legends, Wigginton avoided mirrors and didn't have any in her residence. She avoided sunlight, preferring only to come out at night.

Wigginton would tell her friends that she needed blood to survive and could not eat solid food. She would go to the grocery store and obtain pig's blood which she drank daily for sustenance.

Jervis had taken a drive with Wigginton the Monday before the day they planned to do the killing. Wigginton had rambled on about Satanism and the devil worshiping hierarchy. She informed Jervis that Satan wanted her to be a "destroyer." Then getting all the women together, Wigginton got them all to agree that would find a random victim so that she could "feed."

"(Tracey) was like a shark in a feeding frenzy," Lisa Ptaschinski would say later. "Because of her cravings for blood.

Jervis would say later that she thought the plan was a "joke" but she brought a knife during the drive to find a victim.

What wasn't a joke was that Wigginton would drink the blood of the women in her circle of "vampires".

"I just can't understand how three other woman would follow this other woman with horrific ideas," Gundelach said.

"I said have you seen her drink the blood?" Detective Pat Glancy would ask one of the women during their interrogation. "She said 'I have given her blood. I use my blade that I use for leather work and I slit my veins for her and she sucked the blood from my veins.'"

Wigginton would prefer the blood of Lisa Ptaschinski, drinking her blood but not becoming ill.

"That's a head scratcher," Harding said. "If you drink blood, human blood, you're going to get sick. At a minimum, you're going to be sick to your stomach, literally and figuratively. But this was part of their rebellion. Also remember that vampirism has been noted in psychiatric journals. There are certain people who mistakenly believe that they have this 'need to feed' as Tracey put it. It is a mental sickness. Obviously, a red flag that you're dealing with a psychotic individual. Why these women went along with the program is a indictment on their intelligence."

FINDING THE RIGHT MAN

"They planned to get a man," Detective Pat Glancy said. "That man that they got was poor Mister Baldock I'm afraid."

Two nights after Wigginton declared that she needed to find a "fresh victim", the women gathered up nights and piled into their car, like vampires on a night hunt.

They girls cruised around and found Baldock by sheer choice. He presented a vulnerable target, middle aged with a pot belly and stone cold drunk.

The four women pulled up in their car alongside him, aggressively flirting.

Baldock was feeling lucky as he had just won a dart game over his buddies at a nearby pub. He was a normal average Joe, forty-seven years old with a wife and kids waiting for him at home.

"He was very inebriated when he left (the bar)," Gundelach said. "He had a blood alcohol of .3 percent. So he's an easy victim to lure into the car with four young girls."

Baldock entered the vehicle as the women offered him a lift. Wigginton more than hinted that the girls would provide sex for him.

"There's obviously talk that she's (Tracey) prepared to have sex with him," Gundelach said. "That she'd give him a good time. I think she also indicated that the other girls were available if he felt like them."

The young women drove Baldock down to the secluded banks of the Brisbane river. Wigginton led him out of the car and the two walked to an old boat shed off the water.

"The three waited in the car while Baldock was led down the back (of the shed)," Glancy said.

Wigginton had no qualms in her mind that she would kill Baldock. But she made out with him and got the man to take off his clothes.

She stopped right before penetration, however, and told Baldock that she needed to get something from the car.

Baldock, although drunk, still had his guard up and shoved his wallet under the door of the boat shed so he can get it later.

"He had that sixth sense, I suppose," Gundelach said. "He thought he might be robbed. So he slipped his wallet under the corrugated door under the nearby sign."

Baldock found a loose credit card on the ground. He assumed that it belonged to him as he slipped that under the door with his wallet as well.

"The fact that Wigginton dropped her credit card is a miracle," Harding said. "Psychiatrists thought, and I agree, that somehow, someway that other facet of Tracey's personality came out. That side of her that still had a modicum of right and wrong, the 'Big Tracey' beat out 'Bobby' for just a brief moment. Just long enough to drop the card. A way to self-sabotage her own evil efforts. I shudder to think what would have happened if she didn't drop the credit card. The authorities would have looked for a man or a gang of men. Wigginton and her followers just didn't fit the profile and we would have been left with another unsolved mystery. And they most likely would have gone on to kill again."

Wigginton got back to the vehicle and told the women that she was going to kill Baldock. She got her knife and asked for them to join her.

Only Lisa followed her out as Waugh and Jervis stayed in the car. When Lisa and Wigginton came upon Baldock again, the idea was that they both were going to attack him.

Lisa, however, backed out.

Wigginton didn't.

"I walked around him," Wigginton said. "I took my knife out of my back pocket. He asked me what I was doing. I said nothing and stabbed him...I withdrew the knife and stabbed him on the side of the neck. I stabbed him on the other side of the neck and I continuously stabbed him. I then grabbed him by the hair...and pulled him back, stabbing him in the front of the throat and, at that stage, he was still alive...I stabbed in the back of the neck again, trying to get into the bones, I presume, and cut the nerves. I then sat in front of the tilt-a-doors and watched him die."

Wigginton then ordered Lisa to go back to the car and wait as she drank the man's blood.

Drinking as much as she could, Wigginton then washed up in the river and returned back to the vehicle. The women asked if she had "fed" and she said yes.

Wigginton would never admit blood drinking aspect of the crime to the police.

Her cohorts, however, would be adamant that she drank Baldock's blood. Waugh claimed she smelled blood on Wigginton's breath as they drove back to Jervis' place.

"She looked almost satisfied" Jervis recalled. "Like a person would look if they had just sat down to a three-course diner-which is a gross thing to say."

ONE WOMAN'S BRUTALITY

The sheer violence of the attack left even the most hardened Australian police in shock.

"Tracey stabbed him as hard as she could," Glancy said. "The knife went right to the hilt. She said she got the knife and tried to get into the bones. That was her words. Try to get into the bones."

Wigginton's first stab was into Baldock's back. She nearly severed his spinal cord.

"She stabbed him seventeen or eighteen times according to the pathologist," Gundelach said. "The hole in his back was the largest."

She sliced his throat and then began sucking his blood.

"It was a very depraved and very cruel murder," Gundelach said. "And it's one of the worst."

"When I rolled the body over," said Detective Pat Glancy. "I truly thought the head would detach from the body. It was most uncomfortable."

The young women thought they had gotten away with the murder. The killing was random and there were no witness. But they left behind a clue (the credit) that would have them in custody within hours.

"I don't think we even considered the idea of it (the perpetrator) being female," Glancy said. "We just assumed that it had been done by a man or a number of men."

"It was hard to believe the allegations or the report was true," Gundelach said. "As it turned out everything was true."

"For a short while, at least, Wigginton was able to live out her fantasy," Harding said. "She had visualized that scene of chopping up a man for so long it must have seemed like old hat. That is probably why she was able to go through with a heinous act without the aid of drugs or stimulants like so many other killers. She had built up to this point with her devil worship and wannabe vampire ideas. She become immersed in the darkness so much that everything culminated in that night. She didn't hesitate while the other girls did."

"The irony of her actions is probably lost on her. She spent her whole life rebelling against the church that she was raised in yet the Bible verse 'As a man thinketh, so is he,' is a fitting prophecy of her own life. She thought about darkness everyday, immersed herself in evil and eventually become the embodiment of what she trained herself up to be."

VAMPIRES AND THE MEDIA

The media focused almost exclusively on the vampiric element of the case. Wigginton and the others looked the part with their Gothic clothing and stark, masculine looks.

"She (Tracey) fell in love with the idea of being a vampire," Harding said. "Just like in the movies, the vampire chooses a victim at random. Follows him. Seduces him. And the way they (the young women) dressed like these Goth chicks out for a good time, plenty of cleavage and what have you. Then they killed him and drank his blood. This was all heavily influenced by vampire culture, movies and books. It was all a part of their little fantasy world that they made come to life in the form of killing Baldock."

Furthermore, the media focused a great deal on the lesbian aspect of the murders. Feminists were up in arms as they felt lesbians were being castigated.

"Tracey Wigginton was the dominant in the dating relationships," Harding said. "Lisa was her submissive although it has been said that she was dating Waugh. So there are these open relationships going on and the lurid stories that go along with that. What was lost was that a family man lost his life that night."

A VAMPIRE THAT WILTS UNDER PRESSURE

The four women got together and had an agreed upon story that they didn't see or do anything. Wigginton was arrested within hours of the discovery of the credit card as was Kim Jervis.

Wigginton said that she and Jervis had been at the park during the day and that she recalled seeing a suspicious-looking couple milling around the area. When told that Jervis gave a different story, Wigginton began to wilt. She said that they had, in fact, been at the park at night but they tripped over a body in the dark.

"I had been too frightened to report it to the police," she said after being told that Jervis told the police that they had discovered the dead body at night.

"We walked behind the sailing club," Tracey said. "There we saw the body...it just looked terrible...he had blood all over his face. We just had to get the hell out of there."

Lisa Ptaschinski knew that her friends were being interrogated. She left her home an emotional mess, not knowing whether she should run and hide or just wait.

In the end, she could not bear the anxiety.

She turned herself in at the Ipswitch police station and gave them all the gory details.

Later, Kim Jervis and Tracey Waugh would enter the police station and give their statements on what took place.

SPLIT PERSONALITY?

"She (Tracey) had her story already made up and only admitted things she knew we knew," Glancy said. "It did not worry us but she could unnerve weaker people; a typical psychopathic personality.

Detective Sgt Glenn Burton had a brief but an uncomfortable meeting with Wigginton. He poo-poohed the idea that she had hypnotic powers but he was "impressed with the strength of her personality, a voice which-using two or three words at a time...When she looked at you it was almost as if you didn't exist. It was a stare that went through you."

Prior to the trial, Wigginton was forced to undergo twenty-six hours of hypnosis. She was examined by a couple of different psychologists and psychiatrists who determined that the woman suffered from a multiple personality disorder. It was revealed that she had four different personalities.

Bobby: contemptuous, callous and cynical, the murderous side of her personality.

Big Tracey: anxious and depressed, distressed by the murder, a good personality believed by psychiatrists to have left Wigginton's credit card at the scene of the crime.

Young or Little Tracey: childlike and naïve, who presented Wigginton's childhood days.

The Observer: calm, detached and rational, who acted as a record of the thoughts and actions of Wigginton's other personalities.

They also believe that there was a fifth personality named Avril who was a nightmarish presence that controlled Bobby by "screaming in her head."

All of the four women were brought to trial although none of them took the stand. Videotaped interviews were brought forth instead which revealed the extent of Wigginton's power over the young women in her "coven."

"Tracey has mind power," Waugh said in her interview. "She has a hold on you. She is like a magnet. You can't stop yourself from doing what she tells you to do."

Waugh would become the only defendant acquitted by the jury. Her own attorney described her as a "coward who was vulnerable to Wigginton's manipulations." He also emphasized that Waugh had in fact been Tracey's "reserve victim", that she would be killed in the event that blood could not be found elsewhere.

"Waugh, the most attractive of the three sat demurely with her wide brown eyes downcast," wrote Garibaldi. "Looking the picture of innocence, she prompted the prosecutor to remark that she looked "like a 16 year old schoolgirl."

Jervis' attorney, on the other hand, tried a different tactic. She was described as a "young lady of good character who collects dolls and Garfield cats."

He emphasized the fact that he believed that she was "sucked in" by Wigginton, stating "Wigginton wrote the script, Wigginton wrote the story and she conscripted an extra, my client. Wigginton gave Kim Jervis the chance to step from the audience on to the stage so she could take part in it."

Jervis, however, was found guilty and sentenced to eighteen years despite the fact that she was not on hand for the murder. She had waited in the car with Waugh throughout the killing.

Lisa Ptaschinski, meanwhile, was characterized as an emotional unstable woman who had no idea of the consequences of her actions. Lisa really thought Tracey was a vampire and was a "willing victim" to please Tracey.

"She had a strong attraction," Lisa said. "I don't know what, it's normally very unusual for anyone to push me around. She dominated me more than anyone has in my life."

SENTENCING

In 1991, Wigginton was sentenced to life in prison by the Supreme Court of Queensland with a minimum of 13 years.

Her mother, Rhonda Hopkins, remained angry at the way her daughter was portrayed in the media.

"All I want to get across to people is that she (Wigginton) is not an evil person at all," Hopkins said. "She is not a vampire and she did not drink blood...Tracey is a murderer but she is still a person and she still has rights...It would do a lot to restore Tracey's faith in human nature if she saw the truth printed."

"I remember one time when we had a sick chook and someone told Tracey to chop its head off and put it out of its misery, she couldn't do it. She did not drink blood."

Things did not get much better for Wigginton. In 2006, she attacked another inmate and a prison guard. She lapsed into a depression but found work as the prison librarian.

In 2008, it was rumored that Lisa would be set free from prison after nearly 22 years. Lisa would be released under the resettlement leave program, where she would be given a maximum of 12 hours leave every two months for six months. These reports were later shown to be false.

Jervis would be found guilty of manslaughter and sentenced to 18 years. Her sentence was later reduced to twelve years on appeal.

Waugh would be acquitted of being an accessory.

RELEASE

In her one and only interview, Wigginton expressed remorse for her actions and stated that she has "terrible dreams of his killing."

She stated that she had no connection with Satanism and was herself frightened by the variety of exorcists who met with her at the jail to "rescue her from the devil."

"I was off the planet when I killed," Wigginton said. "I wasn't even my usual doormat self-I was an animal."

She described her killing as a "metaphorical revenge against all those who had hurt her."

"Once I had started (stabbing) I couldn't stop," Wigginton said. "I couldn't see Mr Baldock-I kept seeing my grandmother, my grandfather, my mother, my father and all the people in my life who had hurt me."

Wigginton made numerous unsuccessful parole applications until 2011 when the parole board set her free on January 11th 2012. Her attorney, Josh Fenton, successfully lobbied for her parole as he stated that Wigginton was in such poor health that it was impossible for her to harm anyone once she was released.

He stated that Wigginton suffered from a chronic and debilitating back condition and a knee injury that required crutches for her to walk.

"I don't think she should be released," Glancy said. "I really don't. It was just a vicious crime and done by a woman, a very, very cold calculating woman."

"Murder is a terrifying experience," Wigginton said. "It's extremely scary to have that much power. It's playing God with life and death. Nobody should have that sort of power...but we all do."

D

Louise Melanie "Louise" May was looking for a place to stay.

She had three children but had them taken away as the courts declared her to be an unfit parent because of her drug addiction. At the age of 23, she needed to get her life back together.

Things seemingly could not get any worse for the recovering addict.

But then she arrived at the home of Kerry Dalton seeking help.

"I don't have anywhere to go," Louise said, realizing that her audience in Kerry Lyn Dalton was only half paying attention. "Rob is in jail. They took away my kids. Damn CPS."

The frazzled haired twenty-eight-year-old alternated between staring at the television and smoking on the meth pipe. She took a deep toke on the pipe and let the smoke out.

"You can stay with me," she finally said.

"Oh my God, thank you," Louise said.

"But it is only until Rob gets out," Kerry said.

"I understand. I understand. No problem."

But Louise had a problem. Meth addiction.

Now she had added another problem in Kerry Lyn Dalton.

"Kerry was a queen in the subculture of meth and alcoholism if there is such a thing," forensic psychologist

Greta Smith said. "She had been married twice and had five children by three different men. It was amazing how Kerry Dalton even survived to the age of 28. Unemployable, she was the epitome of a bully and would do anything to get her way. She had little regard for the rights or feelings of other people, running roughshod over everyone in her path."

Unfortunately for Louise, she had gotten in Kerry's way.

Kerry would be arrested for drug possession and hauled off to jail for a short stint. She had been Louise's supplier and Louise needed her fix.

But she had no money.

So she began pawning off things she found around the house during a spur of the moment "garage sales." Some of Kerry's old jewelry would be sold off in exchange for drugs.

But when Kerry was released from prison and found out that her stuff had been pawned off, she became more than livid.

She became homicidal.

"Kerry took the theft as a personal affront," Smith said. "This was a fragile living situation between two drug addicts. Junkies. They had little regard for one another and really see each other as utilities to use or supply drugs. Louise is willing to sell out Kerry's stuff while Kerry is willing to kill Louise to gain revenge."

On June 26th, 1988, Kerry confronted Louise at the mobile home. Three other people in their drug dealing clique soon arrived, Mark Lee Tompkins, Sheryl Baker and another transient named "George".

Kerry ordered Louise to sit down and tied her to a chair. She then began torturing her, splicing off and electrical cord and burning her with it.

Louise screamed in pain.

Tompkins then began joining in the torture, jabbing at the defenseless Louise with a screwdriver.

The two then demanded that Sheryl partake in the abuse as well. Reluctantly, Sheryl complied.

"Sheryl felt as if they would have killed her if she didn't do as she was told," Smith said.

After the course of a few hours, the three then took turns torturing Louise.

Kerry enjoyed shocking her captive with the electric cord, laughing as Louise screamed. Seeking to raise the stakes, her boyfriend took an iron skillet and smashed it against the back of Louise's head.

"They hit her with such force that it made a dent in the pan," Smith said.

Kerry's sadism was still not satiated. She kept thinking of different ways to torture Louise then came up with the idea to inject her with some battery acid. Her boyfriend got a syringe and they plunged the battery acid into her vein as well as poured it down her throat.

"Kerry was a sadist," Smith said. "She justified her torture of Louise to the fact that the woman sold a few items of her jewelry and got maybe twenty-five bucks for it."

Tompkins then put Louise out of her misery by stabbing her in the neck with the screwdriver. She fell to the ground and he began stomping on her head until she died.

What happened to Louise's body after remains shrouded in mystery and hearsay.

Later that evening, a sheriff arrived at the mobile home on a burglary call. He saw no evidence of a burglary but did describe one of the residents, Joann Fedor, as high on meth. The sheriff then inspected the exterior and interior of the mobile home, finding nothing.

The disappearance of Louise remained unsolved for three years until Sheryl Baker had a crisis of conscience. She confessed to the crime, telling the authorities of what happened the day Louise was killed. In return for her confession, the authorities allowed her to plead to second-degree murder.

One of Louise's cousins stated on-line that the prosecuting attorney told her that one of trio involved admitted that they dismembered the body of Louise. They then spread the body parts out across different locations on different Indian reservations.

"For meth heads," Smith said. "They certainly knew what they were doing when disposing of a body. They were all jobless junkies but when it came to murdering someone they were willing to work hard. Damn hard in order to avoid detection. They would have avoided detection but for Sheryl Baker finally coming forward."

Kerry's trial would begin on February 8th, 1995. The judge, Thomas J. Whelan stated that

"I think the record is clear that nobody has ever been found in this case. The record is equally clear that there is circumstantial evidence that there was a homicide. There's also conflicting circumstantial evidence that it may not be a homicide; in fact, she may still be alive ..."

"My reason for making these statements is to establish for the record that in my mind corpus is a legitimate issue in this case. It's not a ruse that - there is a legitimate issue before the jury as to whether or not there's - a corpus of a homicide has been established."

Kerry would never confess to the crime on record and would claim innocence.

"The thing that makes me the most mad is that he is lying, and he knows he's lying," Kerry said of the prosecuting attorney.

The jury foreman, John Castleman, would concede that they found her guilty on the basis of "the type of murder it was" despite a lack of physical evidence to prove that Louise was murdered.

Mark Thompkins would be convicted of first-degree murder.

Kerry Dalton would be sentenced to death on May 23rd, 1995.

"She is the epitome of evil," Smith said. "We can say the drugs did it but there was a lot of premeditation to what she did to poor Louise. If anyone deserves to be on death row and have her execution expedited, it is Kerry Dalton."

Victoria Forbes, however, continues to champion the innocence of her sister.

"She was convicted without a body," Forbes said. "Without a weapon, without any blood evidence, without any physical evidence, without a crime scene, without anyone being declared deceased nearly seven years later as she stood trial with no one declared deceased being charged with the death penalty."

There continued to be some on-line controversy regarding Kerry's guilt as her supporters point to the fact that Louise's husband claims to have had a call from Louise a week after she was murdered.

That "evidence", however, is all they have to go on.

Despite Dalton's persistence at an appeal, it was clear to law officials believe that Kerry Dalton was guilty of the murder of Irenc Louise May. Neither Tompkins nor Baker had anything to go after coming forward after three years of silence. They finally sobered up and confessed their crime.

Kerry Dalton did not and is now on death row.